Escape The Shame Of Babylon

David Webb

Escape The Shame Of Babylon
Copyright © 2025 by David Webb. All Rights Reserved.

All rights reserved. No part of this book may be reproduced in any form or by any electronic or mechanical means, including information storage and retrieval systems, without permission in writing from the Author. The only exception is by a reviewer, who may quote short excerpts in a review.

Cover designed by EKI Publishing

Printed in the United States of America

First Printing: July 2025
Eternal Kingdom International Publishing, LLC
LIBRARY OF CONGRESS
LCCN: 2025942429
ISBN- 978-1-968815-00-4 - Paperback
ISBN- 978-1-968815-01-1 - Hardback
ISBN- 978-1-968815-02-8 - eBook

Copyright © 2025 by Author.
All rights reserved.
Printed in the United States of America

The prophet that hath a dream, let him tell a dream; and he that hath my word, let him speak my word faithfully. What *is* the chaff to the wheat? saith the LORD. *Is* not my word like as a fire? saith the LORD; and like a hammer *that* breaketh the rock in pieces?

- Jeremiah 23: 28-29 (KJV)

Dedication:

This book is dedicated to my family and friends, with whom I have cherished countless moments and shared the knowledge and experiences I have gained in my walk with Jesus Christ.

I extend my heartfelt gratitude to the mentors who have spoken into my life the profound truths of the Kingdom of God. Your teachings went beyond mere words; you provided me with experiences that brought those teachings to life, helping me understand what it means to become a spiritual Father. The time you invested in me was not in vain.

While the full impact of your efforts may only be revealed in time, I know that thousands of lives have been touched and many more reached through your guidance.

I also dedicate this book to those who attended my teachings and encouraged me to transform those lessons into written form.

A special thanks to Hunter (my son), Garrett, Daniel, Chris, Kirkland Rite, and several other friends who patiently read the draft versions of this book and provided invaluable feedback.

David Webb

Introduction

What began as a simple act of obedience - teaching a six-week series at the request of my Pastor - became a divine unveiling I never anticipated. I didn't set out to write a book. I wasn't chasing authorship. I was releasing what God had deposited in me. But something happened.

As I began to teach, the atmosphere shifted. Eyes widened. Pens couldn't keep up. And by the second series, phones were raised, pictures were taken, and hunger filled the room. I felt the weight of it - unfamiliar and uncomfortable at first. I had never seen people respond to teaching like this. But what I thought was a moment was really a movement. They weren't just listening - they were demanding more.

This book was born not out of ambition, but out of divine pressure. The people asked. My Pastor encouraged. And Heaven stirred. So before this class was ever taught live, I wrote it - quietly, secretly as a gift. A surprise offering to those who kept saying, *"There's more in you."* And they were right. There was more. And this is only the beginning. This is territory being claimed.

This book was forged from fire-tested teaching - crafted from prepared notes intended for a class, but destined for something greater. Every page carries the weight of revelation, not theory. And the quotes you'll find throughout? They are not borrowed inspirations - they are direct impartations, lifted straight from the original teaching notes that stirred hearts and shifted atmospheres. This is not recycled content. This is the overflow of divine preparation, now captured in written form for those ready to receive it.

Foreword

By Gerardo Mejia

It was spring 2025 when I first crossed paths with David Webb at an apostolic conference. Pastor Kelly Lohrke was the one who made the introduction—he had that prophetic "nudge" and told us, "You two need to connect." And not just on some casual level—he saw purpose in the friendship.

Since then, David's been super intentional about staying connected. Somewhere along the way, he handed me the book you're holding right now and asked me to read it.

As I flipped through the pages, I could feel his heart jumping off the paper. His love for the Church? Undeniable. His vision? Bold. He's not just dreaming about packed pews—he's dreaming about healthy, growing churches that genuinely love people. He's got a real burden to see churches—especially in the tri-state area—step up and shine, not just for their cities, but as hubs of hope that reach way beyond their zip codes.

This book is more than words—it's a blueprint. And I believe it's going to help a lot of people grow.

Senior Pastor Gerardo Mejia

House of Grace

2413 Greenup Ave, Ashland, KY 41101

https://www.houseofgraceusa.com/.

Foreword

By Dr. James Wright

In David's book, he has given us the keys to how the power of the true Gospel will deliver us from the shame and sins of our past. It's a book filled with Hope, Help, and Healing. He confronts the problems in the church and he powerfully declares the answers. This book will help challenge you and change your life for the better. The bottom line is that we need to stop playing church and totally surrender our lives to our Lord. I highly recommend this book.

By Dr James Wright
Full-Time Evangelist
Wright Way Ministries, Inc.

Foreword

By Ralph Thomas

I have had the distinct honor of knowing David Webb for the past six years. In that time, I've witnessed his walk with God up close—marked by conviction, humility, and a passion for truth. David doesn't just share information; he carries revelation. His life and teaching consistently point others back to the authority of Scripture and the power of the Kingdom.

He has taught classes using these revelatory principles, each one marked by an uncommon depth. David doesn't aim for surface-level inspiration—he presses into the weightier matters of the Spirit. He has a gift not only for helping people identify their spiritual giftings, but also for awakening them—stirring dormant callings and equipping believers to live out their God-given assignments.

Escape the Shame of Babylon is a fiery and fearless call to the Church to come out of compromise and into Kingdom alignment. It exposes the subtle infiltration of the Babylonian spirit—shame, performance-based religion, and powerlessness—that has taken root in modern culture and even crept into our sanctuaries. This book confronts deception, uproots shame, and ignites a bold return to obedience, identity, and spiritual authority. It is more than a teaching—it is a divine trumpet blast for those ready to rise as the remnant.

So, lean in. Let the truth stretch you, convict you, and ultimately set you free. Babylon is falling—and this is your invitation to come out from among it and stand.

By Ralph Thomas
Huntington, WV

Contents

Introduction 9
Foreword 13
  By Dr. James Wright 13
Foreword 15
  By Ralph Thomas 15
Prelude 1
  The Shadow of Babylon 1
Chapter One 5
  The Lie That Bound Us All 5
    The Ancient Whisper: "Did God Really Say?" 5
    Religious Systems Built on Deception 7
    Why the Truth Still Hurts - and Heals 9
    Awakening from the Fog of Babylon 10
    Scripture References: 11
Chapter Two 12
  The Gospel We Were Never Told 12
    From Fire Insurance to Kingdom Invasion 12
    Paul's Declaration of Power (Romans 1:16) 14
    False Comforts, Silent Pulpits 16
    The Cost of Carrying the Real Gospel 18
    Scripture References: 20
Chapter Three 21
  Babylon Is a Spirit, Not a City 21
    The Spirit that Built a Tower 21
    Ancient Babylon vs. Modern Counterfeits 22

    How Babylon Enters the Church 23
    Idolatry, Compromise, and Religious Culture 25
    Discerning the Babylonian System Within 26
    Discerning the Babylonian System Within Your Leadership 28
    Promotion belongs to the Lord, not your man-made testing systems 29
    A Call to Renounce and Rise 30
    Scripture References: 31

Chapter Four 33
    Shame: Hell's Favorite Weapon 33
        When Shame Becomes Identity 34
        Jesus Despised the Shame 36
        Breaking the Agreement with Condemnation 38
        Scripture Reference List: 39

Chapter Five 41
    Religion Won't Save You 41
        The Spirit of Religion vs. the Spirit of the Kingdom 41
        Obedience or Outward Appearance? 43
        Nicodemus at Night: A Picture of Many Today 45
        What Jesus Actually Requires 46
        Scripture References 48

Chapter Six 49
    The Voice of the King 49
        God Is Still Speaking to His People 49
        The King's Word Brings Government 50
        When Truth Confronts the Comfortable 52
        How to Hear and Heed the Voice 53

Scripture References: 55

Chapter Seven 56

Deliverance Is Still for Today 56

Deliverance Is Not A Distraction 56
Jesus Came to Set Captives Free (Luke 4:18) 57
Demonic Influence in the Church 58
Confronting the Strongman 59
Walking in Ongoing Freedom 60
Final Decree: I Am Not Ashamed 62
Scripture References 62

Chapter Eight 64

Obedience Is Not Optional 64

Introduction: The Ancient War for Obedience 64
Submission vs. Religious Performance 65
Jesus: Lord and King, Not Just Savior 66
Obedience Unlocks Access (Hebrews 5:9) 68
Holiness in a Compromised Culture 70
The Call to Uncompromising Obedience 71
Scripture References 72

Chapter Nine 74

The Remnant Rises 74

Biblical Introduction: The Hidden Pattern of Remnants 74
Who Are the Remnant? 75
When the Crowd Leaves, the Called Remain 76
End-Time Boldness 77
Characteristics of the Remnant Church 78
The Rise Begins Now 80
Scripture References: 80

Chapter Ten 82

Repentance – The Forgotten Door 82

What Repentance Really Means (Acts 3:19) 82
Turning from Dead Works 83
From Tears to Transformation 85
The Revival of Repentance 86
Scripture References: 87

Chapter Eleven 88

Truth That Divides 88

A Sword, Not a Feather 88
Why the Real Gospel Offends (Luke 12:51) 89
Division Is a Sign of God's Move 90
False Unity vs. Kingdom Unity 91
How to Stand Firm in the Fire 92
Call to Boldness and Final Declarations 93
Scripture References: 94

Chapter Twelve 95

When Identity Is Rebuilt 95

Reconstructing the Ruins 95
From Orphan to Sonship 96
Knowing Whose You Are 98
Authority Comes from Identity 99
Shame Breaks Where Sonship Rules 100
Scripture References: 101

Chapter Thirteen 103

Walking in Kingdom Authority 103

Introduction: The Kingdom Is Within You 103
Not Just Saved - Sent 104

Power Over Darkness 105
  The Apostolic Mandate of Every Believer 106
  You Are Heaven's Embassy 107
  Reclaiming the Forgotten Authority 108
  Scripture References: 109
Babylon Must Fall 110
  Tearing Down Strongholds 110
  Exiting Cultural Christianity 111
  Calling the Church Out of Egypt 113
  Babylon's Fall Is the Church's Rise 114
  Scripture References: 116

Chapter Fifteen 117
  The Return Home 117
    The Prodigal Nation 117
    Come Out from Among Them 118
    Restored Identity, Renewed Purpose 120
    A Bride Made Ready for the King 121
    Scripture References 122

Chapter Sixteen 124
  The Final Separation 124
    Delivered from Half-Kingdom Thinking 124
    Don't Date Babylon 125
    Non-Negotiables of the Kingdom 126
    The Roll Call of the Unashamed 127
    The Imitation Must Die 127
    Marked for Glory, Not for Compromise 128
    The Echo of the King's Voice 128
    A Divine Encouragement and Final Warning 129

- Scripture References: 130
- Bonus: Chapter Seventeen 131
  - **Obedience To God VS Man** 131
    - Obedience to God Alone: Rejecting the Counterfeit Authority of Men 131
    - Obedience to the Voice of God is Non-Negotiable 131
    - Jesus Christ Exposed False Authority 132
    - Apostolic Teachings Demand Testing of Leaders 133
    - When Obeying Men Means Disobeying God 134
    - Man-Made Leadership Tests Are an Abomination 134
    - Obeying God Means Defying False Authority 135
    - Warning to the Remnant: 136
- Glossary 138
  - of Theological Terms 138
- Index 146
  - **Thematic** 146
- **Scripture Index** 153
  - Old Testament 153
  - New Testament 155

Prelude

The Shadow of Babylon

"The people who walked in darkness have seen a great light; those who dwelt in a land of deep darkness, on them has light shone."
- Isaiah 9:2 (ESV)

Imagine a weary caravan winding along dusty roads toward Jerusalem, the city of promise, after decades of exile in a foreign land. The air hums with hope, yet each step carries the weight of a past that refuses to fade. The Israelites, God's chosen people, return from Babylon, their hearts a tangled mix of anticipation and pain. They have endured unspeakable horrors - young men castrated, their futures stolen; women enslaved, forced into lives of degradation; entire families coerced to bow before false gods under threat of death. These scars, both seen and unseen, cling to them like a second skin, whispering shame and despair. Can you feel it? That heavy burden in your own heart, the shadow of your past mistakes, the wounds of a world that seeks to break you?

In Babylon, the Israelites faced a crucible of suffering. Their initial sin - worshipping false idols - brought divine judgment, as prophets warned, leading to their captivity (2 Kings

17:7-18). In that foreign land, they were stripped of dignity, forced to serve cruel masters and false deities. Yet, amidst this darkness, beacons of faithfulness shone brightly. Men like Daniel, Shadrach, Meshach, and Abednego stood firm, refusing to compromise their devotion to God, even when faced with fiery furnaces and lions' dens (Daniel 3:16-18, 6:10-23). Their courage echoes through Scripture, a testament to God's promise: "Those who remain faithful, I will remember forever" (Isaiah 56:4-5).

Now, standing on the threshold of Jerusalem, the Israelites face a new challenge. The sins and shame of Babylon have seeped into their souls. The men bear physical scars of their mutilation; the women carry the trauma of enforced prostitution. Even the faithful struggle with the weight of their experiences and the fear of judgment from their own people. The community they return to may mock their brokenness or question their worth.

How can they rebuild their lives when shame clings so tightly?

How can they shed the sins - both their own and those forced upon them - to reclaim their identity as God's people?

Yet, God's grace is sufficient. His Kingdom offers a path to redemption, where shame is replaced with honor, sin with righteousness, and despair with hope. The Bible declares, "The Spirit of the Sovereign Lord is on me… to proclaim freedom for the captives and release from darkness for the prisoners" (Isaiah 61:1). This is the promise of God's Kingdom - a realm where the broken are made whole, the oppressed are set free, and the ashamed are clothed in dignity.

This book, Escaping the Shame of Babylon, is your guide to that journey. It is a story of redemption, healing, and restoration, not just for the Israelites but for you. We all carry the shadow of Babylon - whether it's the shame of past sins, the trauma of others' actions, or the weight of societal judgment. Through these pages, you'll discover how to confront your past, embrace God's forgiveness, and step boldly into the purpose He has for you.

The question looms: How can you escape the shame that binds you?

The answer lies in the Kingdom of God, where His light pierces the darkness, and His love transforms the broken.

Chapter One

The Lie That Bound Us All

The Ancient Whisper: "Did God Really Say?"

It began with a whisper. Not in the back alleys of Babylon or on the dusty roads of Jerusalem, but in the untouched purity of Eden. A question slipped through the leaves on the lips of a serpent - subtle, calculated, and fatal: *"Did God really say?"* (Genesis 3:1). In that moment, all of creation was placed on a collision course with confusion. That first lie wasn't about murder or idolatry - it was a direct assault on the clarity of divine truth. The whisper fractured reality, twisted identity, and seeded doubt in the human soul. It wasn't just a lie - it was the birth of Babylon, the spirit of rebellion disguised as reason.

The devil has always preferred whispers to war. False images, false destinations, false definitions. He offers mirages in place of meaning. And just as in Eden, he is still whispering today - not in the ears of sinners alone, but in sanctuaries and pulpits. He speaks through wounded memories, religious routines, and even Scripture twisted out of context. He says you can believe without surrender. That grace is permission. That the Kingdom is optional. But every whisper is a wedge between man and his King.

The devil has been lying to everybody. Not just to sinners, but to saints. Not just to the lost, but to the saved. And the greatest lie is this: you can believe in God and reject His rule. That's the deception that created pulpits of silence and altars of compromise. That's the voice whispering, "You're not enough," or "You'll never be free." It is hell's favorite strategy - undermining the government of God by offering a gospel of comfort with no cross.

The lie never barges in - it whispers. First, it arrives as a subtle suggestion. Then it becomes a thought that lingers. But think on that lie long enough, and you'll begin to move with it. Every sin is born in the mind - conceived in imagination before it's lived in action. And when you repeat the sin long enough, it forms a system - a living code embedded deep inside you, guiding your choices, ruling your habits, and reshaping your identity from within. And soon, believers begin living in agreement with the very lie that enslaved them.

They attend church, sing worship, and quote Scripture - but remain bound. Why? Because until truth becomes personal, it cannot become powerful. You must have your "aha" moment - when light breaks through and exposes the lie you've been living under. Truth must confront before it can heal. And it starts with that one question that still echoes through time: Did God really say?

That's the "aha" moment - when revelation is not just something you hear, but something you become. Until that moment, there is no pursuit. No fire. No realignment. But when truth collides with your spirit, shame begins to unravel.

Babylon thrives in ignorance. The enemy loves silence in the pulpit and numbness in the pew. But the moment truth becomes personal, passivity dies.

Religious Systems Built on Deception

Babylon didn't vanish - it evolved. It put on robes, stepped behind pulpits, and built churches with no government. What began as deception in Eden became doctrine in Jerusalem. When Israel rejected God's rule and demanded a king like the nations (1 Samuel 8:5), they weren't just asking for leadership - they were trading divine order for human hierarchy. This was Babylon creeping into covenant. Every time Israel bowed to Baal, forsook the temple, or ignored the prophets, they weren't just sinning - they were building Babylon brick by brick.

And today, many churches are doing the same. We have pulpits without power. Sermons without surrender. Worship without wonder. We say "Jesus is Lord," but we deny Him rule over our schedules, our spending, and our sexuality. Babylon thrives in religion that honors God with lips but denies Him with living. It allows for passion without purity, form without fire. And it is this religious Babylon that keeps the people bound - while calling it grace.

Most churches are atmospherically rich but governmentally bankrupt. They sing songs to a King they refuse to obey. They gather in His name but reject His commands. Babylon is not absent from the church - it is hosted within it. We don't just flirt with deception - we institutionalize it. And we tell the hurting, the addicted, and the broken that they can belong without transforming. That is not grace. That is captivity in disguise.

The moment you water down the gospel to keep the crowd, you lose the power that could have set them free. Babylon isn't intimidated by a crowd - it's terrified of obedience.

The same spirit that whispered in Eden still whispers today. That's why the only way out is not compromise - it's confrontation. Religion that entertains your wounds but never heals them is Babylonic.

You can't cast out Babylon while trying to win its approval. If your gospel never shakes anyone, it's not the real gospel. If everyone agrees with your message, then you're not preaching like Jesus. He warned, *"Woe to you when all men speak well of you"* (Luke 6:26). The remnant knows - true gospel fire will either provoke deliverance or hostility. But it will never leave you passive.

Why the Truth Still Hurts - and Heals

Paul's declaration in Romans 1:16 slices through the fog: *"For I am not ashamed of the gospel of Christ, for it is the power of God unto salvation."* That's not safe language. It's not comforting. It's confrontational. In Rome, Caesar was called "Lord." So to declare Jesus as King wasn't just theology - it was treason. The gospel Paul preached wasn't about self-help or weekly inspiration. It was about government - an unshakable Kingdom breaking in, demanding surrender and confronting every other authority.

And that's why it still hurts. Because this gospel doesn't negotiate. It doesn't adapt to feelings. It doesn't tiptoe around dysfunction. It shines. It shouts. It exposes. And in doing so, it heals. It doesn't just save from hell - it restores, delivers, confronts, and commissions. The Greek word for salvation - sōzō - means total restoration: of body, soul, purpose, and power. And this is why Babylon fears it. Because when believers begin to align with Kingdom truth, everything built on compromise begins to fall.

This gospel offends before it transforms. It kills before it resurrects. Babylon sells safety. The Kingdom demands surrender.

Paul wasn't whispering in Rome - he was declaring war on every system that resisted the reign of Christ.

This gospel will not make you popular - but it will make you powerful. It will offend before it transforms. It demands the death of your pride so that resurrection power can live through you. Babylon hates it because Babylon cannot control it. And the moment you preach it without shame, demons tremble and systems shake.

This is why Paul also warned in Galatians 1:8-9: *"But though we, or an angel from Heaven, preach any other gospel… let him be accursed."* He repeated it twice for emphasis. The true gospel carries weight. It's not therapy - it's authority. It doesn't just soothe - it sets government in order. And when it is watered down, it loses power and becomes a placebo. But when preached with fire, it produces confrontation and transformation.

Awakening from the Fog of Babylon

The greatest lie still spoken is this: that you can be saved and still live as you please. That the Kingdom is a theory and obedience is optional. But Jesus made it clear: *"Not everyone who says to Me, 'Lord, Lord,' will enter the Kingdom of Heaven, but only he who does the will of My Father"* (Matthew 7:21). You cannot sing about Heaven while living like hell. You cannot preach grace while denying the need for government.

This is the awakening. This is the line in the sand. To be Kingdom is to leave Babylon. To walk in truth is to forsake the lie. And the truth is this: the Kingdom is not a Sunday service - it is a sovereign rule. It is not a feeling - it is a fire. It demands your life, but in return, gives you everything.

Romans 1:16 is not a memory verse - it is a Kingdom decree. To be unashamed of the gospel is to embrace its consequences. When you declare Jesus is King, you declare war on every system - internal and external - that resists His rule. Babylon is crumbling. But only those aligned with the Kingdom will stand.

There is a Kingdom in you that refuses to be silent. A remnant fire that cannot coexist with religion. You don't need applause - you need alignment.

This isn't a dead truth. It's eternal. And it's alive inside you. Don't silence what saved you.

You must decide now: Will you continue playing church in Babylon's system, or will you submit to the government of a holy King? You cannot inherit the Kingdom without renouncing compromise. You cannot follow Christ and ignore His crown. This is not the time to negotiate. It is the time to burn. Come out. Not with hesitation, but with holy boldness. Come out of shame. Come out of false doctrine. Come out of powerless religion. Come out of Babylon - and let the government of the King reign again.

Scripture References:
- Genesis 3:1
- 1 Samuel 8:5
- Luke 6:26
- Romans 1:16
- Galatians 1:8-9
- Matthew 7:21

Chapter Two

The Gospel We Were Never Told

From Fire Insurance to Kingdom Invasion

It began on the slopes of Sinai. The people of God, freshly delivered yet fearfully distant, trembled at the sound of divine thunder and the sight of descending fire. But instead of leaning into intimacy, they recoiled. *"You speak to us, Moses,"* they begged, *"but let not God speak to us lest we die"* (Exodus 20:19). In that moment, a tragic exchange was made. Relationship was traded for religion. Fire was forfeited for form. And instead of a Kingdom of priests, a priesthood of one was appointed. Thus, religion was born not in reverence, but in fear.

God spoke not with sentiment, but with supernatural force. Sinai wasn't a conference. It was a confrontation. God wasn't offering poetry - He was issuing decrees. This was not therapy; this was authority. The people wanted inspiration and affirmation only, but God offered them invasion. They rejected rulership for ritual.

What God intended as a divine invasion became man-managed insulation. And this tragedy has echoed through the centuries. Even now, pulpits thunder with clichés but tremble to proclaim government. We were told to prepare for evacuation, not occupation. We packed our bags for rapture, not rulership. But the

King never asked for spectators - He called for sons, ambassadors, and co-rulers. We were not saved to sit. We were saved to govern.

You were not born for comfort. You were born for confrontation. You were not redeemed to hide - you were born to invade. The Gospel we were never told was not about escaping earth, but transforming it. Heaven isn't waiting for us to leave. It's waiting for us to lead.

Some of you were told to prepare for rapture, not rulership. You packed your bags to escape, not to engage. But God says: "Unpack your rapture bag. We are going to be here a while." Why? Because He's not coming until the job is done. And the job is to preach-not man's opinion, not denominational tradition-but the eternal Gospel of the Glorious Kingdom of unshakable authority and peace (Matthew 6:33, Romans 14:17).

Over seven billion souls are waiting - hungering - for truth before the King returns. The earth is not silent; creation itself is groaning with anticipation. Romans 8:19 declares it boldly: *"For the earnest expectation of the creature waiteth for the manifestation of the sons of God."* Heaven is watching. Earth is waiting. And the sons of God must rise and speak - the world cannot be reached by silence.

Find someone or look in a mirror and say, "He's not coming till we do the job." What job? The job of government. The job of alignment. The job of delivering cities, discipling nations, and restoring families. The city can be saved - if the church can be saved. Your house can be delivered - if you will be delivered first.

This gospel we were never told - it breaks atmospheres. It doesn't negotiate. It doesn't adapt to culture. It shifts it. When it is declared, not explained, the air changes. The earth responds. Demons retreat. Power is released. Because this gospel is not just information - it's invasion. It doesn't just ask for agreement - it demands surrender.

The anointing has limits - yes, limits. If it were without boundaries, then Jesus Himself would have turned every priest, every heart in Israel, and every ruler in Rome. But He didn't. And yet, today's preaching often claims the anointing is limitless, ignoring reality and embracing a seductive illusion. Many boast, "I have the anointing - I can break anything." But the true measure was never in your shout - it was in your impact on culture. You were called to shift culture, not echo it. So how far did you truly go in transforming the people in the world around you? That is the measure of your leadership.

Those trapped in this deception are not just misled - they're blind. They've lost the fire of divine vision. The ancient wisdom still speaks: *"Where there is no vision, the people perish: but he that keepeth the law, happy is he."* (Proverbs 29:18). Vision anchors the soul, but deception unravels it.

Paul's Declaration of Power (Romans 1:16)

Paul, the fire-branded apostle, thundered across the Roman Empire with a bold decree: *"I am not ashamed of the gospel of Christ, for it is the power of God unto salvation to everyone who believes"* (Romans 1:16). But this was no safe slogan. In a world where Caesar was god, to declare another King was sedition. This gospel was not therapeutic - it was governmental. And Paul knew its weight.

When Paul wrote "Christ," the Hebrew mind would hear Messiah - not just Savior, but King. And to the Jewish people who had endured Babylon, Assyria, and now Rome, Messiah meant restoration of dominion. Not just spiritual revival, but political, cultural, societal transformation. And yet, when Jesus came, there was no outward revolution. The Kingdom did not come with chariots, but with a cross. It did not come to crush Rome but to crucify self. And because of that, many rejected it.

The moment you say "Messiah," you're declaring war on systems. You're dethroning idols. The Kingdom is not a suggestion - it is a takeover. Most Christians want the Kingdom on their own terms, but that mindset has built denominations that divide instead of unify. That's why churches war with churches down the street. That's why pulpits compete instead of conquer. We have churches atmospherically rich but governmentally bankrupt.

Romans 1:16 is not a memory verse. It is a Kingdom decree: *"For I am not ashamed of the gospel of Christ, for it is the power of God unto salvation."* Paul was writing to the Romans - the elite, the powerful, the first-world thinkers of his day. To them, 'Messiah' was not a spiritual term. It was political. It was disruptive. To say

Jesus was Messiah meant declaring a new King, a new government, a new order.

And Paul, without flinching, says: "I'm not ashamed of that message." Because he knows it carries Kingdom weight and demands Kingdom loyalty.

But hear this: If Paul, who had seen Heaven and encountered Christ Himself, had to wrestle with the temptation to be ashamed, how much more must we? He called it paralyzing shame that whispers unworthiness. That's the shame that tells you: "Don't preach that." "Don't be identified with that message." It's not just embarrassment - it's spiritual warfare. And Babylon thrives on it.

In the American church, this shame has created pulpits of silence and altars of fear. We preach benefits without repentance. We offer blessings without obedience. But the eternal gospel is not just about what God gives - it's about what He requires. It has a positive side and a negative side. Like a battery, it carries both the power to spark life and the shock of conviction.

False Comforts, Silent Pulpits

The American Church has become fluent in benefit but mute in responsibility. We preach "give and it shall be given" but forget to mention what happens if you rob God. We sing of blessing but whisper about obedience. We promote grace but tiptoe around holiness. And in doing so, we have given people the crown without the cross, the robe without the repentance.

The gospel of salvation says you go to Heaven when you die. But the gospel of the Kingdom says Heaven invades your now. If your gospel doesn't shift culture, it's not His. If your gospel doesn't confront demons, it's counterfeit. If your gospel doesn't produce authority, it's irrelevant. The American Church has been trained to say "Amen," but not to obey.

This gospel we were never told has consequences. Because the true gospel is not a slogan - it's a sword. Jesus Himself declared, *"Do not think I came to bring peace, but a sword"* (Matthew 10:34). Why? Because truth always divides. The gospel that saves also offends. The message that heals also exposes. And until we return to preaching the full counsel - the blessings and the boundaries - we will have churches full of members but void of citizens.

Let's go deeper. The word 'salvation' in Romans 1:16 is *sōzō* - a word that means more than going to Heaven. It means deliverance from demons. Healing from brokenness. Restoration of destiny. And most people don't even know what they need until this gospel exposes the hole in their spirit. The power of *sōzō* is restoration in every dimension. But that restoration doesn't come to spectators. It comes to those who align with the voice of the King.

The Cost of Carrying the Real Gospel

Here is the truth: if you're preaching the real gospel, people will either run to you or run from you. But they will never remain neutral. Jesus said, *"Woe to you when all men speak well of you, for so did their fathers to the false prophets"* (Luke 6:26). The real gospel makes devils scream. It makes sinners cry. It makes lukewarm leaders angry. And it makes Heaven stand at attention.

Some of you have felt it - that urge to shrink back, to soften the blow, to blend in. That's not humility. That's shame. And shame silences boldness. The devil knows he can't destroy you, so he paralyzes you. He whispers: "Don't preach that." "Don't identify with that message." And the moment you comply, you start your descent into compromise.

Let me tell you about the first time something broke inside me. I wasn't in a church. I wasn't at the park witnessing to people handing out Gospel tracts. I found myself standing across from a warlock - a real one. His eyes full of rebellion, he looked at me and said, 'If I had your hair, I could curse you.'

In that moment, the Spirit of God whispered, 'Give it to him.' If this gospel doesn't work now, don't wait until you die to find out. So, I reached up, pulled a few strands of my own hair, handed it to him, and said, 'Do what you can'

But after I walked away, I began thinking to myself. I wonder if his curse will work. I don't feel any different. Why was I thinking like this? Because I have never been cursed, and I did not know how it felt to be cursed. I was curious and a little nervous. When you are learning, you think about these kinds of things.

A week passed. I saw him again at the mall. I walked up and said, 'I'm still here, and I'm still covered in the blood of Jesus.' And he began to shake - tremble like something was crawling inside him, similar to an epileptic fit.. I realized something in that moment: I wasn't just surviving - I was tormenting a tormentor.

Something changed in me. I wasn't ashamed anymore. Not of tongues. Not of deliverance. Not of the gospel that still works. I had become unashamed - and I was dangerous.

This is why Paul said, 'I am not ashamed.' Because the very moment shame enters in, your descent begins. Shame silences boldness. Shame makes you passive. Shame separates you from the authority that drives demons out and heals cities.

So shout it. Preach it. Post it. Prophesy it. Raise your kids in it. Choose your relationships by it. If they can't be loyal to the King, they won't be loyal to you.

Listen. In this moment, God is walking the aisles of your heart. Angels are taking names. There is a roll call of the unashamed. Can He count you among the bold?

Because revival isn't coming to the clever. It's coming to the courageous. Miracles are not falling on the trendy - they're falling on the loyal. And the King is not seeking talent - He's seeking alignment.

Let the fire fall. Let the gospel be preached. And let the nations see the glory of the King. Amen.

Scripture References:
- Exodus 20:19
- Romans 1:16
- Matthew 4:17
- Matthew 10:34
- Matthew 6:33
- Matthew 6:22-23
- Galatians 1:8-9
- Psalm 26:1-2
- Luke 6:26
- Luke 9:23
- 1 Corinthians 4:20
- Romans 14:17
- Ephesians 5:25-27
- Revelation 19:7

Chapter Three

Babylon Is a Spirit, Not a City

The Spirit that Built a Tower

In the ancient plains of Shinar, humanity first came together under one rebellious banner - not to glorify God, but to build a name for themselves. The city of Babel, founded by Nimrod, was not just a place - it was a declaration. *"We will ascend... we will make a name for ourselves..."* (Genesis 11:4). But Heaven responded, not with applause, but with scattering. The confusion of languages was more than a judgment on their speech - it was a disruption of a counterfeit spirit. That spirit didn't die with the tower. It became Babylon.

Babylon, in Scripture, is not merely a location. It is a spiritual system - a counterfeit kingdom. It appears in Daniel's visions, dominates empires, and is still alive in the book of Revelation. It wears religious garments while sipping from cups of abomination. It is both ancient and modern. It has no address but controls cities. Babylon is a spirit. And that spirit hates the rule of God.

Today, Babylon moves through politics, entertainment, education, and even pulpits. It seduces saints with compromise, lures leaders with influence, and cloaks deception in religious language. But this chapter is a trumpet blast to the remnant: Babylon must fall - not just around us, but within us. Because Escaping Babylon begins with discerning its spirit. Babylon is a spirit of substitution. It offers religion without relationship, comfort without consecration, crowds without covenant. It will let you say the name of Jesus, as long as you deny His rule.

Ancient Babylon vs. Modern Counterfeits

Babylon's origin in Genesis was rooted in pride and rebellion. It was man saying, We don't need God's direction - we'll build our own way to Heaven. That same spirit animates today's culture. Babylon is not extinct. It has evolved.

Modern Babylon appears more refined, more palatable. It dresses in self-help slogans, political ideologies, religious traditions, and entertainment. It does not mind your attendance in church, as long as your allegiance remains with culture. It's the system that teaches believers how to function in dysfunction without ever breaking free.

The spirit of Babylon is alive wherever there is mixture. Mixture of truth and lies. Of faith and fear. Of worship and idolatry. Revelation 17:1-6 describes her as a seductive woman, drunk on the blood of the saints, riding on a beast of deception. She doesn't demand you renounce Christ - just that you redefine Him. That you adjust the gospel to fit your feelings.

The church has entertained Babylon long enough. When churches preach blessing but ignore repentance, when leaders water down the gospel to remain popular, when people seek spiritual experiences but reject spiritual authority - we are no different than Israel in exile, singing the Lord's song in a foreign land (Psalm 137:4).

Babylon is not limited to ancient ruins or prophetic metaphors - it is a living, breathing spirit that whispers through the systems of this world. It sits on the shoulders of the depressed, rides in the minds of the double-minded, and whispers to every part of your soul that resists the order of God.

Demons don't die - they just recycle people. That same spirit that spoke in the Garden still whispers today. And many believers don't even know what they need until this gospel exposes the hole in their spirit.

Scripture reminds us that *"friendship with the world is enmity with God"* (James 4:4). Babylon is the world's spirit systemized. And if we embrace it, we reject the Kingdom.

How Babylon Enters the Church

Babylon doesn't break down the front door. It seduces through the side entrance of compromise. It starts with subtle shifts in language: calling sin a "struggle," calling conviction "judgmental," calling obedience "legalism." The pulpit, once a place of fire, becomes a platform of performance.

The spirit of Babylon infiltrates worship when emotion replaces truth. It saturates sermons that entertain but never confront. It thrives where deliverance is replaced with therapy, and the Holy Spirit is treated like a mascot instead of the Governor of the Kingdom.

Paul warned Timothy of a time when people would not endure sound doctrine but would gather teachers who say what they want to hear (2 Timothy 4:3). That time is now. Babylon enters when we prioritize crowds over covenant, relevance over reverence, and convenience over consecration.

Bluntly: You can't partner with Babylon and pray like Zion. You must choose your allegiance. Either the Spirit of God governs you, or the system of Babylon does.

Many churches, unknowingly, are preaching a gospel that accommodates those demons. A gospel without cost. A gospel without transformation.

And it doesn't stop with the church. Babylon targets families. It redefines marriage. It sexualizes children. It exalts self above sacrifice. It thrives in every environment where the government of God is absent.

Jesus warned in Matthew 15:8-9, *"These people honor Me with their lips, but their hearts are far from Me. They worship Me in vain; their teachings are merely human rules."* Babylon thrives in that kind of worship-performance without presence.

Ezekiel 22:26 says, *"Her priests do violence to My law and profane My holy things; they do not distinguish between the holy and the common..."* That's Babylon in the pulpit: no distinction, no discernment, no fire.

Idolatry, Compromise, and Religious Culture

Idolatry is not bowing to statues - it's bowing to ideas that replace God. Babylon's system exalts image over intimacy. It creates platforms instead of altars. It breeds spiritual influencers who market holiness while living in hidden sin.

Compromise is Babylon's native language. It teaches that holiness is optional, that truth is subjective, and that obedience is extreme. It is the doctrine of mixture - offering just enough truth to keep you pacified, but not enough to set you free.

Religious culture is Babylon in disguise. It sings songs but rejects surrender. It builds cathedrals but forgets the cross. It quotes Scripture but refuses repentance. And worst of all, it learns to perform Kingdom behavior while resisting Kingdom transformation.

God is not fooled. He sees through the fog of religiosity. He is calling for a church that tears down idols, confronts compromise, and rejects the religious show for a genuine Kingdom encounter. Babylon must be cast out - not catered to.

Babylon cannot bless you. It can only entertain you. But Zion transforms you. Babylon numbs your senses with religion and noise. Zion awakens your spirit with power and purity.

Zion declares: "You are not called to manage dysfunction - you're called to crucify it. You're not called to survive Babylon - you're called to destroy its hold on your life."

Isaiah 1:13-17 exposes this false religious performance: *"Stop bringing meaningless offerings! Your incense is detestable to Me... I cannot bear your worthless assemblies... Wash and make yourselves clean. Take your evil deeds out of My sight!"* Babylon offers empty rituals. The Kingdom demands transformation.

Romans 12:2 calls us not to conform to this world but to be transformed by the renewing of our minds. Babylon conforms; the Kingdom transforms.

Discerning the Babylonian System Within

This war is not just external - it is deeply internal. Babylon isn't just out there - it's in here. In our motives. Our fears. Our secret allegiances. And unless we let the Spirit of Truth expose it, we will carry Babylon into every place we are called to bring the Kingdom.

You can't cast out Babylon if you're still feeding it. You can't confront a system that you're still benefiting from. Babylon whispers through wounded memories and unhealed places. It tells you to protect your image instead of walking in truth. It convinces you that agreement is love and confrontation is hate.

But Kingdom people are different. They don't fear the fire - they walk through it. They don't echo culture - they confront it. They don't negotiate with devils - they cast them out. To discern Babylon is to identify every belief, behavior, or system in you that opposes the rule of Jesus.

Discerning Babylon requires radiant light that exposes every hidden thing. It takes boldness to ask, "Where have I compromised?" It takes humility to admit, "I've aligned with the wrong kingdom." And it takes courage to say, "Babylon, you no longer have my allegiance."

You can't process betrayal with a carnal mind. You can't forgive by flesh alone. You need the Holy Spirit to grant you grace, prophetic wisdom, and radiant light that exposes every hidden thing.

It reminds us: "The enemy isn't intimidated by your attendance - he's terrified of your transformation." And "your story is not your trauma. Your destiny is not your dysfunction. You are not shaped by who left or who failed you - but by the God who stayed."

Ephesians 6:12 reminds us, *"For we wrestle not against flesh and blood, but against principalities, against powers..."* Babylon is not just emotional - it is spiritual. It must be discerned and cast down with Kingdom authority.

Psalm 139:23-24 is our cry: *"Search me, O God, and know my heart... See if there is any offensive way in me, and lead me in the way everlasting."* The true remnant asks to be searched, exposed, and reformed.

Discerning the Babylonian System Within Your Leadership

So, you want to measure your relationship with God's people versus the religious Babylon that still lives in your leadership? Regardless of whether you're a layman in the church or the Senior Pastor, look no further than the evidence of your fruit. If you are struggling in an area of your public ministry.

The Peter Principle exposes the truth: "You were promoted to the highest level of your incompetence." And instead of raising up competent sons and daughters, you surrounded yourself with weaker vessels - because their weakness protected your pride. That is why your ministry is struggling.

You were never meant to build alone. You were supposed to train, equip, and release others with as much - if not more - competence than yourself. But you refused to steward what the Lord entrusted to you. You buried the talents in fear, insecurity, or selfish ambition, and now you blame the warfare on others. Yet it was *you* who would not build, *you* who would not train, and *you* who would not multiply.

Promotion belongs to the Lord, not your man-made testing systems.

God never asked you to invent new methods of control - He commanded you to raise up sons and daughters. Fathers prepare their children for the future - they do not abandon them, creating orphans, they do not compete with them, they do not destroy their destinies, and they do not steal children from other houses, what God never assigned to them. When you kidnap the spiritual sons of another house because they carry what you never cultivated, you expose your barrenness. You failed to labor and reproduce, now wanting to manage someone else's harvest.

And if certain areas of your ministry function better without your presence, you should be weeping before God - not celebrating. If you rejected the raw, humble package that the Lord gave you because it didn't look like the polished imitation you saw on someone else's stage, you've become a clone factory - producing images without breath. *That* is the mark of a leader governed by Babylon. You're chasing forms without power, titles without function, charisma without covenant, and reproducing without the correct DNA.

You cannot manufacture what God knit into another man's DNA. You cannot reproduce an anointing that Heaven never assigned to you. You cannot fake divine design.

What God births is Holy. What Babylon duplicates is hollow. Leadership is not about control - it is about covenant, competence, and crucifixion. If you can't die to your own ego, you'll never raise up a generation that lives.

When you elevate people based on appearance or charisma - because you like how the package looks or sounds, you're not building a kingdom; you're building a stage for Saul and entertainment in the style of Babylon. That's how you end up with performers, not kings. God is not impressed with the wrapper - He's searching for the substance. You need those who walk in the gifts, not those who merely talk about them. Their presence becomes a divine signal - revealing the traps ahead, and guiding you to the better path.

But if you ignore that wisdom, what you're really doing is feeding lust to entertain the crowd. It's no different than hosting a spectacle - like a bikini contest. Yes, it'll draw attention. Yes, the room will be full. But it won't be full of anything Holy. It won't be filled with transformation. And it certainly won't birth revival.

A Call to Renounce and Rise

Babylon is not a city. It is a system. A spirit. A seductive structure that hates surrender. But it has already been judged. Revelation declares, *"Fallen, fallen is Babylon the Great..."* (Revelation 18:2). Its end is certain. But until then, we must come out.

"Come out of her, My people, lest you share in her sins..." (Revelation 18:4). This is not a suggestion - it's a command. And it requires more than church attendance. It demands full Kingdom allegiance.

So rise, remnant. Tear down the idols. Cancel the compromise. Confront the religion. Cast down the mixture. And let the fire of God burn Babylon out of you. Because only then can you walk in the authority, purity, and power of the unshakable Kingdom.

Babylon is falling - but only those aligned with Zion will stand. Let every spiritual contract with compromise be broken. Let every agreement with apathy be revoked. Let every lie be cast out. And let the Kingdom rise.

You cannot break agreement with Babylon while still seeking its approval. This is the war between boldness and shame.

Hebrews 12:28-29 reminds us: *"Since we are receiving a Kingdom that cannot be shaken, let us be thankful, and so worship God acceptably with reverence and awe, for our God is a consuming fire."*

Babylon is a spirit - but the Kingdom is a fire. Let it burn.

Scripture References:
- Genesis 11:4
- Daniel 2-5
- Revelation 17:1-6
- Revelation 18:2
- Revelation 18:4
- Psalm 137:4
- James 4:4
- 2 Timothy 4:3

- Matthew 15:8-9
- Ezekiel 22:26
- Isaiah 1:13-17
- Romans 12:2
- Ephesians 6:12
- Psalm 139:23-24
- Hebrews 12:28-29

Chapter Four

Shame: Hell's Favorite Weapon

The Voice That Says You're Not Enough

From Eden to now, the enemy has wielded shame like a weapon - not with steel and fire, but with whispers. In the garden, Adam and Eve hid not because of God's anger but because of shame's voice. That voice still echoes today, whispering, "You're not worthy. You're too broken. You're too late." It isn't just a feeling; it is a full-on assault against your identity. Shame is not just the aftermath of sin; it is the strategy of hell.

The Devil has been lying to everybody."And the most effective lie is not one shouted from the mountaintop, but one whispered in the darkness of our minds. That whisper doesn't just say you're wrong - it says you're worthless. It doesn't just accuse your actions - it condemns your essence. And here's what you must understand: shame is not guilt. Guilt says, *"I did something wrong."* Shame says, *"I am something wrong."* (2 Corinthians 7:10)

That is hell's objective. Not just to tempt you, but to tether you. Not just to wound you, but to brand you. So that every time you rise to pray, every time you lift your hands in worship, that voice chimes in: "Who do you think you are?" And if you believe it, you stop contending. You stop pursuing. You stop preaching. And that is when hell wins.

Shame is the voice that keeps you quiet when God calls you to speak. Shame keeps you seated when Heaven tells you to stand. It is the suffocating darkness that veils hearts - the internal sabotage that paralyzes prophets and silences warriors. Shame doesn't come from God. Shame doesn't convict - it cripples. And many believers have made an unholy agreement with shame, and it accuses them. (Revelation 12:10)

Paul understood this. He declared in Romans 1:16, *"I am not ashamed of the Gospel of Christ, for it is the power of God unto salvation."* Why make such a bold statement? Because even he felt the pull - the spiritual warfare of shame that says: *"Don't be identified with that message."* And if Paul had to wrestle with it, you better believe we do too.

In this moment, get this!!! That means if it's the right Gospel, it will cause paralyzing shame that whispers unworthiness. The word shame means to feel disfigured, to feel disgraced, to feel rejected. Here's the big one: To feel, "I don't want to be identified with that message."

When Shame Becomes Identity

The tragedy of the modern church is not just that people sin. It's that they live as sin. They wear it like a cloak. They adopt the identity that hell assigned to them. They speak from pulpits while shame whispers in their soul, "If they knew who I really was, they'd never listen." And they lead, sing, preach - all while hiding in fig leaves of performance.

But hear this: Shame is a liar. It is a false prophet. It speaks with religious tones and trauma echoes, but its message is hell-born. And when it goes unchallenged, it becomes your lens. You begin to interpret every correction as rejection, every delay as dismissal, every hardship as divine punishment. And worst of all, you start agreeing with it. (Proverbs 23:7)

Truth becomes powerful when it becomes personal. Until you confront the lie that says, "You're not enough," you will never walk in the authority that declares, "Christ is more than enough in me." Identity in Christ is not a theory. It is a violent rejection of every counterfeit label. When Jesus tore the veil, He tore off the voice of shame. He didn't just save your soul - He silenced your accuser. (John 8:11; Romans 8:1)

You are not going to be passionate and pursue the things of God until that moment of revelation. Until shame is exposed and renounced, you will be a spectator to your own calling.

Yet too many believers live as if the veil is still intact. They hide behind shame-soaked religion, afraid that exposure will destroy them. But exposure to truth doesn't destroy - it delivers. You were never meant to live half-lit, half-loved, half-free. The eternal Gospel, alive with Heaven's thunder and urgency, does not negotiate with shame. It confronts it. It casts it out. It replaces the whisper of unworthiness with the roar of righteousness.

You are not what you did. You are not what they said. You are not the failure, the addiction, the divorce, the secret. You are who He says you are. (2 Corinthians 5:17; 1 Peter 2:9) And that means shame has no more legal right to speak into your future.

Jesus Despised the Shame

"Looking unto Jesus, the author and finisher of our faith, who for the joy that was set before Him endured the cross, despising the shame..." (Hebrews 12:2).

There it is. Jesus *despised* the shame. He didn't ignore it. He didn't carry it. He confronted it. He shamed the shame. And how did He do it? By embracing the cross *naked*. And Jesus also did it openly, the scripture tells us this:

Colossians 2:15 *"And having spoiled principalities and powers, he made a shew of them openly, triumphing over them in it."*

Let that sink in. The King of Glory, the Word made flesh, hung on a Roman cross with nothing to hide Him. No loincloth, no fig leaf, no robe of righteousness. He bore your shame by becoming completely exposed. Why? Because He had to redeem what Adam lost in Eden. And Adam lost glory the moment he put on shame. (Genesis 3:7-10)

Jesus took the shame so you could wear the glory again. (Isaiah 61:7)

This is not poetic. It is prophetic. He was dishonored so you could walk in honor. He wore thorns so you could wear a crown. He took your shame, not just so you wouldn't feel bad, but so you could rise up, speak up, stand up, and never again bow to hell's favorite weapon.

And yet today, we apologize for bold preaching. We get quiet about deliverance. We silence tongues. We hide healing. Why? Because we're ashamed. Not ashamed of sin - we're ashamed of the power of the Gospel. That's the disease. We want a polite church. Quiet deliverance. A Gospel with no blood, no fire, no noise. (2 Timothy 3:5)

But Jesus didn't die politely. He died violently. And He rose victoriously. And He left no room for shame to stay standing. So, if He despised shame, why do you entertain it?

In this moment watch this…. He became poor so that we may become rich. He became naked, that we may be clothed. He received dishonor that we may have honor. He got a crown of thorns, that we may have a crown of life! He was bruised for our iniquity! (Isaiah 53:5; 2 Corinthians 8:9; Revelation 2:10)

Let someone boldly declare: "I'm not ashamed of the eternal Gospel, alive with Heaven's thunder and urgency of Jesus Christ!"

Breaking the Agreement with Condemnation

Here is the secret few will say out loud: **shame is a covenant.** It is an agreement of identity, sealed by experience, fueled by silence. And it must be broken.

You don't cast out shame with a self-help book. You sever it at the altar. You renounce it like a demon. You say, "I break agreement with shame. I break agreement with condemnation. I break agreement with every voice that says I'm not enough."

Agreement is authority. Whatever you agree with, you empower. That's why demons look for permission. They don't care how loud you shout if you still believe their lie. But when you cancel the contract, their legal access ends. The curse cannot stay where the cross has been applied. (Ephesians 4:27; Colossians 2:14-15)

Some of you were raised in performance-based religion. You were taught to serve for love instead of from love. And that doctrine soaked your soul in shame. But the Kingdom is not built on performance. It's built on presence. *"This is My beloved Son in whom I am well pleased."* That was said before Jesus did a single miracle. (Matthew 3:17)

So today, the Spirit of the Lord is inviting you to break the contract. Rip it up. Call it what it is. Shame is not your accountability partner. It is your spiritual oppressor. You don't need to manage it. You need to evict it.

You cannot walk in Kingdom authority while holding hands with condemnation. Shame is not humility. It's pride in reverse. It's self-obsession covered in self-pity. And it must die.

The moment you become ashamed of the eternal Gospel, you lose the impact of the Gospel for your generation. So today, choose your weapon. Silence or fire. Shame or righteousness. Compromise or conviction. Because the Kingdom doesn't coddle your insecurity - it crowns your surrender. (Philippians 3:13-14; Romans 8:15)

Because the moment you are ashamed, it starts your descent into mediocrity and a suffocating darkness that veils hearts. Let every voice of condemnation be silenced. Let the accuser be cast down. Let the sons and daughters rise with fire in their eyes and thunder in their voices and declare:

"I am not ashamed. I am not unworthy. I am not broken. I am chosen, redeemed, and bold. I will not bow to shame. I will not agree with hell. I will walk in the freedom of the Son." (Galatians 5:1; John 8:36)

Because shame has a voice. But now, so do you.

Scripture Reference List:

- Romans 1:16
- Hebrews 12:2
- Genesis 3:1-10
- Matthew 3:17
- Revelation 12:10
- Isaiah 61:7
- Isaiah 53:5
- Psalm 34:5
- Galatians 5:1
- John 8:11

- John 8:36
- Romans 8:1
- Romans 8:15
- 2 Corinthians 5:17
- 2 Corinthians 7:10
- 2 Corinthians 8:9
-

- 1 Peter 2:9
- Proverbs 23:7
- Philippians 3:13-14
- Colossians 2:14-15
- Ephesians 4:27
- 2 Timothy 3:5

Chapter Five

Religion Won't Save You

The Spirit of Religion vs. the Spirit of the Kingdom

There is a reason the modern church is exhausted: it has been trained to perform instead of obey. When power is absent, performance increases. But God never called His people to perform; He called them to partner. Partner with His voice. Partner with His Spirit. Partner with His Holiness. The anointing is not a theatrical effect - it is the evidence of alignment.

When the early church preached the gospel, it wasn't followed by applause - it was followed by fire, miracles, imprisonment, or riots. Because the Kingdom is confrontational. It shakes cities. It breaks chains. It exposes false systems and topples idols. That same spirit is moving now, seeking those who will not be ashamed of the gospel of the Kingdom - who will shout it even if it costs them everything.

The devil has been lying to everybody. Not just to those who are addicted or lost in immorality - but especially to those sitting comfortably in pews. Religion has become the sanctuary of deception. Babylon has built its altars not just in cities, but inside sanctuaries, on platforms decorated with lights and smoke, delivering polished sermons void of the cross. The spirit of religion is not the absence of God - it is the substitution of His voice for tradition.

Paul's roar in Romans 1:16 must become our echo: "I am not ashamed of the gospel of Christ: for it is the power of God unto salvation to everyone that believes." He wasn't just defending theology - he was declaring war. When Paul used the term 'Christ,' he wasn't offering a devotional title. 'Christ' in Hebrew understanding meant Messiah - the coming King, the restorer of divine rule. Saying 'Christ is King' meant Caesar is not. It meant man's systems must crumble, and God's order must prevail.

This is why the true gospel provokes shame. The Spirit said, 'I will break the shame off the gospel being preached in the church.' That shame is the whisper that says, 'Don't be too loud, too bold, too strange. Stay safe.' But safe preaching saves no one. Real Kingdom preaching divides the room. You either burn or bolt. It's not neutral. If the gospel you preach makes everybody comfortable, it's not the gospel of the Kingdom - it's Babylon in disguise.

God is not looking for performers. He is looking for alignment. And where the Spirit finds agreement with the Word, power is released. 1 John 5:7-8 declares, *"There are three that bear witness... the Spirit, the water, and the blood: and these three agree in one."* When the message and the messenger align with heaven, atmospheres shift, demons flee, and souls awaken. Agreement is more than saying 'amen' - it is walking in full surrender to divine government.

This gospel includes judgment as well as joy, repentance as well as restoration. And just like a car battery needs both positive and negative to generate power, the truth of God needs the fire of both mercy and holiness. We must stop preaching half-truths and calling them grace. Grace that doesn't lead to obedience is deception in disguise.

Obedience or Outward Appearance?

The gospel doesn't accommodate the flesh - it crucifies it. When we preach Jesus as an add-on instead of Lord, we rob Him of His throne in people's hearts. The Word says, *"Walk in the Spirit and you shall not fulfill the lust of the flesh"* (Galatians 5:16). This means holiness isn't optional - it's a lifestyle of constant death to the carnal and resurrection into divine life.

Some believers have been taught to behave but never taught to surrender. They think conviction is condemnation and confuse emotion for repentance. But when God truly shows up, conviction burns like a cleansing fire. It leaves no idols standing. It purifies intentions. And it produces a life that no longer just attends church - but becomes the Church.

Religion says, 'Look holy.' The Kingdom says, 'Be crucified.' Religion is an expert in aesthetics - it will teach you how to clap on beat and smile while secretly suffocating under shame.

Jesus rebuked the Pharisees, not because they weren't devout, but because they weren't obedient. *"Woe to you, scribes and Pharisees, hypocrites! For you are like whitewashed tombs..."* (Matthew 23:27). You can be decorated on the outside but dead on the inside.

We've built services designed to impress people, not host the King. Lights, fog machines, clever quotes - but no brokenness. We cry during worship yet never repent during the Word. And so the Spirit lifts, and all that remains is emotional residue. But when God finds a people who will not perform but obey, He comes in fire.

Luke 6:46 cuts to the soul: *"Why do you call Me 'Lord, Lord,' and not do what I say?"* This is not theological trivia - it is a divine indictment. The Lord isn't looking for churchgoers. He's looking for dead men walking - believers crucified to opinion, ego, and applause.

Religious people say, 'Just be nice.' Kingdom people say, 'Let truth reign.' And truth, when declared in fire, offends before it transforms. That's why Jesus said, *"Woe to you when all men speak well of you"* (Luke 6:26). If everyone loves your message, it's probably not His message.

There should be a reaction. 'If people only look at you with passive faces, something is wrong.' When the gospel is preached correctly, it pierces. It ignites repentance. Or it exposes resistance. But it never leaves people the same.

Nicodemus at Night: A Picture of Many Today

Nicodemus represents the well-dressed seeker - the man who wants answers but not accountability. The woman who craves truth but hides her transformation. But Jesus refuses to whisper salvation into your secret life. He requires you to step into the light and make a public declaration. Romans 10:10 says, *"With the heart one believes unto righteousness, and with the mouth confession is made unto salvation."*

There are too many undercover believers, trying to follow Jesus without upsetting their circle. But the Kingdom is not quiet. It's not hidden in a corner. When light comes, it exposes. When truth is revealed, alignment must follow. The invitation is open - but the terms are not negotiable.

Nicodemus was not a casual seeker. He was a respected leader, a ruler, and teacher of Israel. Yet he came to Jesus at night. Why? Because religion had conditioned him to seek truth in private while preserving image in public. This is the tragedy of modern Christianity - private conviction but public silence. We want light, but not exposure.

Jesus didn't pamper his intellect. He bypassed debate and went for the jugular: *"Unless one is born again, he cannot see the Kingdom of God"* (John 3:3). Nicodemus had spent his life mastering Scripture, but he was blind to the Spirit. Knowledge without birth produces pride. But the Spirit births clarity, obedience, and fire.

Nicodemus came by night because religion had trained him to hide. But Jesus invited him to die. *"You must be born of water and the Spirit"* (John 3:5). This wasn't metaphorical - it was governmental. It meant death to status. Death to silent spirituality. Death to compromise. The Kingdom isn't for seekers of comfort - it's for those willing to lose everything.

This is our indictment. We love sermons that inspire, but we flinch when they convict. We crave revival but avoid repentance. We want Kingdom crowns without Kingdom crosses. But until we are willing to lose our reputation, our platform, and our place in religious systems, we will never carry the fire of Heaven.

Nicodemus is the prototype of American Christianity - respected, intelligent, and neutered. But Jesus is still calling men and women out of the shadows, into the fire, where rebirth is not symbolic - it's supernatural.

What Jesus Actually Requires

The power of the gospel isn't just what it delivers you from - it's what it delivers you into. Into divine identity. Into righteous government. Into purpose that cannot be shaken. If your gospel doesn't transform your priorities, it's not the gospel Jesus preached.

You cannot be neutral and carry the gospel. You cannot serve two kingdoms. You must renounce the throne of self and bow to the government of Christ. That's why Jesus didn't say, 'Add Me to your life.' He said, 'Follow Me.' That call still echoes today - not to half-hearted believers but to fire-branded disciples who cry aloud: I have decided to follow Jesus. No turning back. No turning back.

What does Jesus require? Everything. This gospel demands full surrender - not just of behaviors, but of belief systems, emotional idols, cultural preferences, and religious mindsets. It's not behavior modification. It's identity crucifixion. *"If anyone desires to come after Me, let him deny himself..."* (Luke 9:23).

This gospel is not soft. It does not tolerate mixture. It doesn't negotiate with idols. It casts them down. That's why Paul was unashamed - because the gospel was not his opinion. It was God's order. It worked, not because it sounded good, but because it was aligned with Heaven.

'Demons don't die. They recycle people.' And they thrive in religious spaces where the gospel is stripped of power. If your sermon comforts demons, it isn't from the throne. If your leadership platform protects rebellion, it's built on sand. True Kingdom preaching burns up everything that resists divine rule.

The church does not need more clever communicators. It needs crucified carriers. Men and women who do not flinch. Who do not apologize. Who will weep between porch and altar, and then roar with fire in their bones. The time for mixture is over.

So cry aloud. Declare it in the streets. Post it. Preach it. Prophesy it. 'I am not ashamed!' If it saved you, you must speak it. If it delivered you, you must decree it. Because this gospel - the one with fire and thunder - is not just a message. It is the King's decree, and it still works.

Scripture References
- Romans 1:16
- 1 John 5:7-8
- Matthew 15:8
- Matthew 23:27
- Luke 6:46
- Luke 6:26
- Matthew 7:21
- Luke 9:23
- John 3:3-5

Chapter Six

The Voice of the King

God Is Still Speaking to His People

From the burning bush to the thundering cloud of Sinai, the God of Scripture is a speaking God. When He speaks, creation responds. He spoke and light exploded out of nothing. He breathed and man became a living soul. On the Mount of Transfiguration, the Father's voice broke through the cloud declaring, *"This is My beloved Son. Hear Him!"* (Luke 9:35). At Pentecost, the sound of a rushing mighty wind marked the arrival of the Holy Spirit and prophetic utterance. When Jesus appeared to John on Patmos, His voice was like the sound of many waters (Revelation 1:15). The God of both covenants is a speaking King. But in every generation, humanity has wrestled with the same decision - will we listen to His voice, or will we settle for a substitute? Babylon always offers an alternative voice - one more palatable, more polite, and powerless. But the Kingdom advances through proclamation. And the voice of the King still thunders.

The earliest refusal of His voice birthed religion. "*Moses, you speak to us instead*," Israel pleaded at Sinai (Exodus 20:19). That moment began a pattern of human preference for proxy. We would rather hear from a man than bow before the King. But this chapter is a call back to the fire. A call to realign with the voice that shakes temples and splits seas. A call to recognize that God still speaks - not just in poetry, but in power.

The purpose of the preaching of the Gospel of the Kingdom is to activate Kingdom living where we become the salt and the light, we affect everything else. He speaks through the Word, through the Spirit, and through the prophetic voice that echoes through the chambers of the surrendered soul. But make no mistake - He is not whispering sweet suggestions. He is releasing decrees. His voice is not background noise; it is government. And it demands a response.

The King's Word Brings Government

The Gospel of the Kingdom is not merely good news - it is a regime change. When the King speaks, He establishes dominion. That's why Jesus didn't begin His ministry with an invitation to therapy. He began it with the declaration, *"Repent, for the Kingdom of Heaven is at hand"* (Matthew 4:17). Repentance isn't sorrow. It's a change of alignment. A shift in government.

"If I don't receive the Gospel of the Kingdom where government comes into my life, and Jesus is not just my Savior, He's my Master, He's my Lord, He's my Governor, He is my King. Then my life will fall apart".

The Lord's Prayer doesn't say, "Your church come." It says, *"Your Kingdom come. Your will be done, on earth as it is in Heaven"*

(Matthew 6:10). That is a governmental prayer. That is a surrender to divine legislation. When Jesus taught His disciples to pray, He was not giving them a religious formula. He was training them to invoke the rule of God over every domain of life - over sickness, over sin, over systems.

Whisper the word Government. What does the King do? He governs. Your government come and your will be done.

God's Word is not a suggestion - it is a sword. It cuts. It divides. It conquers. Hebrews 4:12 declares, "*For the word of God is alive and active. Sharper than any double-edged sword... it judges the thoughts and attitudes of the heart.*" The King's word brings correction, conviction, and commission. And when we receive it rightly, we don't just feel better - we come under order.

So what happens when the King speaks? Atmospheres shift. Demons tremble. Sick bodies heal. Bound souls break free. When Jesus cast out demons, He didn't negotiate - He commanded. When He called Lazarus forth, death relinquished its grip (John 11:43). When He spoke to the storm, nature obeyed (Mark 4:39). Luke 11:20 says, "*But if I with the finger of God cast out devils, no doubt the Kingdom of God is come upon you.*" That's the power of the King's voice - it doesn't ask for agreement; it demands submission. I remember a moment in prayer when I heard Him say, "Call them out by name." I obeyed, and within moments, deliverance erupted in the room. The voice of the King is not merely audible - it is transformational.

When Truth Confronts the Comfortable

The problem with modern religion is not that it lacks voices - it's that it lacks the right voice. We have preachers, influencers, and authors who can articulate ideas, but where is the voice of the King? Where is the piercing truth that shatters deception? The eternal Gospel - alive with Heaven's thunder and urgency - is not therapeutic. It is governmental. It does not entertain; it confronts.

Do I need to sing you a song to get the medicine to go down? A spoonful of sugar helps the medicine go down. Nobody got saved by Mary Poppins, and you don't ride Chitty Chitty Bang Bang to Heaven.

Too many believers want Kingdom benefits without Kingdom confrontation. But truth that never challenges is not truth - it's flattery. Jesus never offered a Gospel that left people the same. He declared, "*I am the way, the truth, and the life. No one comes to the Father except through me*" (John 14:6). That's not a slogan. That's a sovereign declaration. And it confronts every other voice.

Jesus said "Pick up your cross! And follow me!" He told one guy to sell his inheritance if he wanted to be his disciple!

Some will say, "Don't preach that - it's too extreme. People will be offended." But the Gospel is not meant to comfort the unrepentant. It is meant to awaken them. The voice of the King does not stroke egos; it resurrects dead men. And resurrection always begins with a burial. If your Gospel never calls you to die, then it's not His Gospel.

We have become ashamed of the Gospel. And that's why we're not having the effects of the Gospel!

How to Hear and Heed the Voice

God is still speaking. But are you listening? Not with carnal ears, but with spiritual discernment. Revelation 2:7 declares, "*He who has ears, let him hear what the Spirit says to the churches.*" There's a difference between hearing and heeding. Many heard Jesus, but only a few followed. The rich young ruler heard the call - but walked away. Mary sat at His feet while others busied themselves with tasks. The voice of the King is not always loud - but it is always clear. And those who train their ears in obedience will hear what others miss. The sheep know His voice, not by volume, but by intimacy (John 10:27).

To hear Him rightly, you must be surrendered. God doesn't speak to impress; He speaks to instruct.

Demons don't die. They just recycle people.

Hearing the King begins with the Word. Scripture is the foundation of all prophetic clarity. Any voice that contradicts the Word is not His. But from that foundation, the Spirit gives instruction - specific, personal, powerful. He convicts, corrects, and commissions. And when He speaks, He expects obedience.

James 1:22 says, "*Be doers of the word, and not hearers only, deceiving yourselves.*" Partial obedience is disobedience. Delayed obedience is disobedience. The voice of the King does not invite suggestions. It issues commands. And those commands bring life.

"The Gospel of the Kingdom is full of absolutes."

There are moments when God will speak through a whisper. And there are moments when He will shout through a prophet. But the key is not volume - it's posture. Are you listening with reverence? Are you ready to respond? Because the greatest insult to a King is not disobedience - it's indifference.

Jesus had several kinds of meetings. For the congregation, for the 70, for the leaders. He didn't say everything he knew to everybody he knew.

We must return to the fear of the Lord. That Holy Awe that says, "*Speak, Lord, for your servant is listening*" (1 Samuel 3:10). That trembling obedience that refuses to filter His voice through cultural trends. That radical surrender that says, "Even if it costs me everything - I will obey."

This is your moment. Not just to hear - but to heed. Not just to receive inspiration - but to enter into alignment. Because the voice of the King is not optional. It is essential. And when you say yes, everything changes.

So rise, remnant. Let there be no more delay. Tear down every idol. Silence every counterfeit voice. Shake off the dust of complacency and step into divine alignment. The King's decree is going forth - who will answer? Lift your voice like a trumpet, lift your hands in surrender, and declare with boldness: "I will obey the voice of the King. I will walk in the power of His Word. I will carry the fire of His Kingdom." This is the hour. This is the summons. Respond - not with hesitation, but with Holy resolve.

So lift your voice. Say it boldly: "I hear the King."

And then live like it.

Scripture References:

- Luke 9:35
- Revelation 1:15
- Exodus 20:19
- Matthew 4:17
- Matthew 6:10
- Hebrews 4:12
- John 11:43
- Mark 4:39
- Luke 11:20
- John 14:6
- Revelation 2:7
- John 10:27
- James 1:22
- 1 Samuel 3:10

Chapter Seven

Deliverance Is Still for Today

Deliverance Is Not A Distraction

In the days of Jesus, the synagogues were filled with religious words but not Kingdom power. They had scrolls without freedom, priests without fire. And then, one Sabbath in Nazareth, the Messiah stood up, opened Isaiah, and thundered: *"The Spirit of the Lord is upon Me, because He has anointed Me to preach good news to the poor. He has sent Me to proclaim liberty to the captives..."* (Luke 4:18). In that single moment, the King declared war on bondage. He didn't come to negotiate with demons. He came to cast them out.

Deliverance was not a side ministry. It was central to the Gospel of the Kingdom. The same Jesus who taught in parables also rebuked spirits, silenced strongholds, and drove devils into pigs. And He passed that same authority to us: *"These signs shall follow those who believe: in My name they will cast out demons..."* (Mark 16:17). Yet today, many churches are too polite to confront what Jesus came to destroy.

This chapter is a confrontation. A prophetic cry that deliverance is not outdated or optional. The ministry of setting captives free is not an extremist agenda - it is the evidence that the Kingdom of God has arrived. *"But if I cast out demons by the finger of*

God, surely the Kingdom of God has come upon you" (Luke 11:20). Deliverance is not a distraction - it is a demonstration. And we must recover it now.

Jesus Came to Set Captives Free (Luke 4:18)

The mission of Jesus wasn't therapy - it was total transformation. He didn't come to manage dysfunction. He came to evict it. When He declared in Luke 4:18 that He was sent to set the captives free, He wasn't being poetic. He was exposing the core assignment of His Kingdom: liberation. From shame, sin, sickness - and demons.

Deliverance is not an embarrassment. It's the evidence of God's government invading a fallen world. The eternal Gospel, alive with Heaven's thunder and urgency, shakes chains loose the moment it's declared. When Jesus preached, people were healed, demons screamed, and atmospheres shifted. If that's not happening in your church, then something has gone missing.

"Demons don't die; they just recycle people." This piercing truth shatters the illusion that deliverance is outdated. The same spirits that tormented souls in ancient days still linger, looking for entry points - through trauma, rebellion, bitterness, and sin. And Jesus came to evict every one of them. Not hide them behind religious curtains. Not anesthetize them with self-help slogans. Evict. Expose. Expel.

This is why preaching the Gospel without deliverance is incomplete. *"For this purpose the Son of God was manifested, that He might destroy the works of the devil"* (1 John 3:8). And yet the modern church, in an effort to appear respectable, has traded deliverance for decorum. But the eternal Gospel doesn't need a soft voice and a fog machine. It needs unashamed proclamation. It needs fire.

Demonic Influence in the Church

Let's be brutally honest: demons go to church. In fact, they prefer religious environments that deny their existence. Because where there's no confrontation, there's no eviction.

The spirit of Babylon loves to attend services. It dresses up, sings songs, quotes verses, and whispers, "Don't stir anything up. Just let people feel good." But the Kingdom of God is not about emotional sedation. It is about spiritual invasion. You cannot make peace with a strongman and expect freedom.

Some churches have perfected the art of religious performance without power. They have exchanged tongues for timidity, and deliverance for dignity. But Jesus never held back when He saw demonic oppression. He rebuked spirits in synagogues (Mark 1:23-26). He delivered the tormented in cemeteries (Mark 5:1-15). And He never apologized for the disruption.

If devils never scream in your church, it's not because they're absent - it's because they're comfortable. They are not bothered by songs that don't carry authority. They are not moved by sermons that avoid truth. But the moment the eternal Gospel, alive with Heaven's thunder and urgency, is declared, something begins to shift. Conviction pierces. Darkness trembles. And demons lose their grip.

Many believers are unknowingly influenced by demonic patterns. That secret addiction? That cycle of shame? That inner voice saying, "You'll never be free"? It's not just psychological - it's spiritual. You can't counsel out what needs to be cast out. You can't pacify what must be pierced with truth.

Confronting the Strongman

You can't take territory without facing the strongman. I once stood with a young man whose family had been oppressed by addiction for generations. When he began to walk with God, everything seemed fine - until we prayed about his family. He started to convulse, growl, and speak in a voice that wasn't his. It wasn't just emotional - it was spiritual. We weren't dealing with behavior. We were confronting a strongman that had ruled his bloodline. When we called it out and broke agreement with its lies, he was set free, and his whole family began to change. That's the power of confronting the strongman. Jesus said plainly, *"No one can enter a strong man's house and plunder his goods, unless he first binds the strong man"* (Mark 3:27). There are strongholds ruling over cities, churches, and families - because no one has dared to confront the strongman.

Deliverance begins where agreement ends. As long as you partner with the lies of the enemy, the door remains open. But the moment you declare, "I break agreement with fear, shame, rebellion, pride…" - that's when the eviction notice is posted. You don't manage demons - you cast them out. You don't negotiate with oppression - you rebuke it.

Too many believers are trying to be nice to what needs to be destroyed. But the Kingdom doesn't advance through politeness. It advances through power. Paul said, *"The Kingdom of God is not in word, but in power"* (1 Corinthians 4:20). That power is not theory - it's deliverance.

Let this be clear: the strongman over your bloodline is not intimidated by attendance. He's intimidated by alignment. When your voice aligns with Heaven, when your hands stretch forth with authority, when your life becomes an altar - then the strongman starts shaking. Then territory is reclaimed.

Walking in Ongoing Freedom

Deliverance is not just a moment - it's a movement. It's not just about what happens at the altar - it's about how you live after the altar. I remember counseling a woman who had just experienced deliverance at a revival service. She was radiant, but two weeks later, she called in tears. The freedom she had felt seemed to be fading. We talked, and it became clear - she had returned to the same environment, the same friends, the same music that had fed her old struggles. She hadn't filled her life with truth. So we made a new plan: daily Scripture reading, worship filling her apartment, a new community of believers to walk with her. And week by week, she regained her footing. Because freedom requires formation. Jesus didn't just cast out demons. He told the delivered, *"Go and sin no more."* In other words, stay free.

Ongoing freedom requires ongoing agreement. You must reject the lies every day. You must close every back door of compromise. That old thought pattern? Crucify it. That toxic relationship? Sever it. That secret sin? Drag it into the light. Because freedom is maintained through obedience.

"Walk in the Spirit, and you shall not fulfill the lust of the flesh" (Galatians 5:16). This isn't about perfection - it's about posture. Are you leaning toward the King or toward your cravings? Are you feeding your freedom or entertaining your demons?

Deliverance is a doorway - but discipleship is the path. Some want the demon gone but not the discipline. But if you don't fill the house with truth, the old spirits will return - with reinforcements (Matthew 12:43-45). Freedom without formation becomes a revolving door.

You must learn to weaponize your worship. Let your house be filled with the Word. Let your car be saturated with prayer. Let your friendships be fortified by truth. Because the Kingdom doesn't just cast demons out - it keeps them out.

Final Decree: I Am Not Ashamed

This Gospel still works. It still delivers. It still confronts darkness and disarms devils. And we are not ashamed of it. We are not ashamed of crying out. Not ashamed of demons coming out. Not ashamed of falling on our faces before the King. Because we know the truth: *"Where the Spirit of the Lord is, there is liberty"* (2 Corinthians 3:17).

So raise your voice. Lift your hands. Let hell hear it. "I am not ashamed of the eternal Gospel, alive with Heaven's thunder and urgency!" I declare it over my life. Over my house. Over my church. Over my city. Let the fire fall again. Let deliverance roar again.

Because deliverance is not a footnote in the Gospel - it is the headline. It is the thunder that breaks chains. The sword that slays deception. The movement that tells Babylon: your reign is over.

Deliverance is still for today. And so is freedom.

Scripture References

- Luke 4:18
- Luke 11:20
- Mark 16:17
- 1 John 3:8

- Mark 1:23-26
- Mark 3:27
- 1 Corinthians 4:20
- Galatians 5:16
- Matthew 12:43-45
- 2 Corinthians 3:17

Chapter Eight

Obedience Is Not Optional

Introduction: The Ancient War for Obedience

In the earliest days of creation, obedience was never meant to be optional. In Eden, a single instruction was given, not as a test of willpower but as a revelation of allegiance. And yet, the serpent hissed a question that still echoes today: "Did God really say?" Obedience is not about rules. It is about rule. It reveals who you trust, who you submit to, and whose government you belong under. The fall of man was not just disobedience - it was defection. It was the original sin of choosing independence over intimacy. And ever since, Babylon has whispered the same old song in new forms: "God understands. It doesn't take all that. You can still be blessed and disobedient." But Heaven has never changed its stance: obedience is alignment, and alignment is access.

From Genesis to Revelation, obedience has been the defining mark of Kingdom citizens. In every generation, God has looked for a remnant - not just of believers, but of obeyers. Faith that does not obey is fantasy. Love that does not submit is a lie. We are not saved because we obey; we obey because we are saved. We have made obedience optional in our pulpits, our parenting, and our politics. But the Word does not bend to our culture. The Gospel does not beg for agreement. It declares war on rebellion. And in this chapter, we will declare the absolute: Obedience is not optional.

Submission vs. Religious Performance

The church has mastered performance. We know how to lift our hands, nod our heads, and amen the preacher. But God is not impressed by external display. He sees alignment. Babylon trains people in religious performance. It teaches them how to appear godly without surrendering to God's government. You can dance, prophesy, serve, and preach - and still be a rebel in the spirit.

Jesus rebuked the Pharisees not for lack of passion, but for misplaced loyalty. *"These people draw near to Me with their mouth, and honor Me with their lips, but their heart is far from Me"* (Matthew 15:8). Babylon doesn't mind your church attendance, your volunteering, or your songs - as long as your heart refuses to bow. Submission is deeper than behavior. It is spiritual positioning. You can speak in tongues and still live in flesh. You can prophesy and still partner with darkness. The test is not gifting - it's agreement.

The Kingdom demands more than activity. It demands authority. And authority only flows through alignment. You cannot cast out devils with a defiant heart. You cannot walk in power while rejecting the process. You cannot lead others when you have not been led. That's why submission is the real test. Because it exposes the heart.

Religion trains you to perform. The Kingdom trains you to obey. And that obedience will often confront your feelings, your comfort, and your logic. That's when the war begins. Because obedience is not an emotion - it's a decision to bow when you want to run, to agree when you want to argue, to yield when your flesh wants control.

Submission isn't about weakness - it's about government. And government is what Babylon hates. Babylon wants a church full of talent but void of order. It celebrates gifting while tolerating rebellion. But God is raising a remnant who understand: submission is not bondage. It is placement. It is protection. It is power.

When you ignore submission, you invite deception. Just like the serpent whispered in Eden, the devil thrives where alignment is absent. And many are falling because they know how to sing about Jesus but refuse to serve Him. The atmosphere of Babylon rewards performance. But God responds to order. It's not the noise that moves Heaven - it's the agreement.

Jesus: Lord and King, Not Just Savior

We have preached a half Gospel. A Gospel that emphasizes salvation but ignores surrender. A Gospel that offers Jesus as Savior but not as Lord. But the Bible is clear: *"That if you confess with your mouth, 'Jesus is Lord,' and believe in your heart that God raised Him from the dead, you will be saved"* (Romans 10:9).

Lordship is not a bonus feature. It is the entry point. Jesus is not your spiritual consultant. He is King. And a king does not give suggestions - He gives decrees. In Babylon, Jesus is a mascot. In the Kingdom, He is Monarch. The difference is not in the name, but in the obedience. "Jesus is not asking for your applause. He is demanding your allegiance." The modern church has tried to rebrand Him into a comforting figure who blesses without confronting. But the Gospel that avoids the King's Lordship is no Gospel at all - it is Babylon in disguise.

Everywhere Jesus went, He preached one message: *"Repent, for the Kingdom of Heaven is at hand"* (Matthew 4:17). He did not invite people to attend church - He commanded them to enter government. And government requires obedience.

We cannot claim His blood and deny His rule. We cannot sing "I surrender all" while negotiating our terms. The Kingdom is not a democracy. It is not run by votes or popularity. It is ruled by a King whose word is law. And He said, *"Why do you call Me, 'Lord, Lord,' and do not do what I say?"* (Luke 6:46).

Obedience is not legalism. It is love. *"If you love Me, keep My commandments"* (John 14:15). In Babylon, love is emotion. In the Kingdom, love is allegiance. You cannot say you love Him and consistently disobey Him. Grace does not eliminate obedience. Grace empowers it.

Jesus is not looking for weekend fans. He is building a government of surrendered sons and daughters. People who say, "Not my will, but Yours be done" even when it costs them everything. Because in the Kingdom, love is not proven by what you feel. It's proven by what you obey.

And we must say it clearly - many are calling Jesus their Savior, but not living as though He is their King. If you reject His design, you reject the King who designed it. If you reject His commandments, you reject His authority. This is not semantics - it's surrender. Either He governs your life or Babylon does. There is no middle ground. You cannot serve two masters. You must choose.

Obedience Unlocks Access (Hebrews 5:9)

There are levels of access in the Kingdom. Not everyone walks in the same authority. Why? Because authority is tied to obedience. *"And having been perfected, He became the author of eternal salvation to all who obey Him"* (Hebrews 5:9).

Notice the qualifier: *"to all who obey Him."* Not to all who listen. Not to all who believe. But to those who *obey*. Obedience is the access point. It is the bridge between revelation and manifestation.

You can have the Word memorized but still be powerless if you won't obey it. You can have prophecies, dreams, and confirmations - but if you won't move when God says move, you stay locked out of the very thing He showed you.

Obedience is a key. It doesn't just unlock miracles - it unlocks identity. When Jesus was baptized, the Heavens opened, and the Father declared, *"This is My beloved Son, in whom I am well pleased"* (Matthew 3:17). What had Jesus done at that point? No miracles, no crowds, no sermons. Just obedience. And the Heavens opened. "Obedience realigns the soul, grants access to divine strategy, and gives angels permission to move on your behalf." This isn't passive spirituality - this is Kingdom transaction. Every obedient act sends a ripple through the spirit realm.

Some of you are waiting for God to open the Heavens, but you won't open your heart. You want access without alignment. Power without submission. Blessing without responsibility. But Heaven does not endorse rebellion. It rewards obedience.

Every time you obey, something opens. Every time you say yes when it's hard, you access more. More revelation. More authority. More joy. More fire. The greatest enemy of access is not Satan. It is stubbornness. The glory does not fall where rebellion reigns.

Jesus told us that the man who built his house on the rock was the one who heard and *"did"* what He said (Matthew 7:24). Revelation without application is deception. And many are drowning in storms not because they didn't hear - but because they refused to obey.

Holiness in a Compromised Culture

We live in a compromised culture. Holiness is mocked. Purity is outdated. Obedience is seen as oppression. But God is still Holy, and His people must be Holy too. *"As obedient children, do not conform to the evil desires you had when you lived in ignorance. But just as He who called you is Holy, so be Holy in all you do"* (1 Peter 1:14-15).

Holiness is not a personality trait. It is a spiritual posture. It is agreement with God's nature. Babylon says you can be saved and still live dirty. The Kingdom says you are saved to be clean.

Obedience produces holiness. Not the fake kind that hides in religious clothes and big Bibles. It is not how you cut your hair or brush your teeth, trim your beard, or shave it off. But the kind that shows up in integrity, humility, and purity. The kind that doesn't just avoid sin but loves righteousness. "Holiness is not behavior management - it is war against compromise." Holiness is not legalism. It is alignment with God's character. It is the separation that breaks spiritual agreements with Babylon and establishes spiritual jurisdiction for Kingdom dominion.

A compromised culture needs a consecrated Church. Not louder slogans. Not flashier lights. But lives marked by obedience. Your obedience is a prophetic act. It declares to the world: "I am not of this system. I am governed by another King."

You can't change a world you resemble. If you talk like Babylon, dress like Babylon, party like Babylon, and date like

Babylon - you can't call others to the Kingdom. Holiness is what separates you. Obedience is what marks you. Purity is what preserves you.

Let the world call it radical. Let the religious call it legalism. Let the lukewarm call it too much. But let Heaven say, "Well done, good and faithful servant."

God is looking for a Holy people, not a popular people. If you still need the world's approval to feel significant, you're not yet dead to Babylon. When you live Holy, you live free. And when you obey God fully, hell has no legal right to your destiny. The enemy's power is broken where holiness is chosen.

The Call to Uncompromising Obedience

The time for suggestion-based Christianity is over. The hour demands absolutes. Heaven is not looking for attendees - it is recruiting ambassadors. People who obey without delay. Saints who bow even when it's unpopular. Warriors who say yes when it hurts.

Obedience is not about perfection. It's about direction. It's about saying, "God, I will not delay. I will not debate. I will not dilute Your voice." As Scripture declares, *"Whoever claims to live in Him must live as Jesus did"* (1 John 2:6). And when you live like that, the atmosphere around you shifts. Demons recognize your authority. Angels move at your word. The Heavens respond.

This is the hour of obedience. This is the rise of those who don't just believe, but obey. Who don't just attend, but advance. Who don't just speak Kingdom, but live Kingdom.

So, let every other voice be silenced. Let every excuse be cast down. Let every part of you rise into alignment. Because obedience is not optional. It is the oxygen of the Kingdom. *"To obey is better than sacrifice, and to heed is better than the fat of rams"* (1 Samuel 15:22).

Say it with fire: "I will obey. I will submit. I will follow the King - even if no one else does."

Because in this war between Babylon and the Kingdom, obedience is your weapon, your badge, your access, and your proof. *"Blessed rather are those who hear the word of God and obey it"* (Luke 11:28).

The Gospel does not need your applause - it demands your alignment. You don't just believe it with your mouth; you prove it with your obedience. So let it be said of you: And when the King returns, may He find you not just believing - but obeying.

Scripture References

- Genesis 3:1
- Matthew 15:8
- Romans 10:9
- Matthew 4:17
- Luke 6:46
- John 14:15
- Hebrews 5:9
- Matthew 3:17
- Matthew 7:24
- 1 Peter 1:14-15

- 1 John 2:6
- 1 Samuel 15:22
- Luke 11:28

Chapter Nine

The Remnant Rises

Biblical Introduction: The Hidden Pattern of Remnants

Throughout the unfolding pages of scripture, a divine pattern emerges: when the multitude bends to idolatry, God preserves a remnant. When the nation drifts into compromise, God raises a voice in the wilderness. From Noah to Elijah, from Jeremiah to John the Baptist, the remnant is God's answer to rebellion. These are not the loudest or most celebrated. They are the hidden, the faithful, the forged in fire. Isaiah cried, *"Unless the Lord of hosts had left to us a very small remnant, we would have become like Sodom, we would have been made like Gomorrah"* (Isaiah 1:9). God always leaves Himself a witness. Even when the temple is in ruins, even when the nation has forgotten His name, He preserves a people within the people. And in this hour, that remnant is rising.

They are not found in the spotlight but in the secret place. They are those who refuse to sell their birthright for cultural comfort. Romans 11:5 confirms, *"Even so then, at this present time there is a remnant according to the election of grace."* Elijah cried out in despair, thinking he was alone, but God responded, *"I have reserved for Myself seven thousand men who have not bowed the knee to Baal"*

(Romans 11:4, 1 Kings 19:18). The remnant may appear outnumbered, but they are never outpowered. They carry the weight of divine preservation and the assignment of generational course correction. The Lord has always used a few to shift the direction of the many. Just as He used Gideon's 300, so He uses His remnant today. They are Heaven's enforcement agents of the Kingdom.

Who Are the Remnant?

They are not the crowd. They are not the cultural Christians who gather out of routine or religious duty. The remnant is a prophetic people, marked by obedience, not popularity. They have not bowed to Baal. They have not kissed the feet of compromise. They live with a fire that cannot be explained and a loyalty that cannot be purchased. "Jesus is coming for a bride that is not a little girl... that's a full-grown woman... and one without spot, wrinkle, or blemish." The remnant is that bride, matured through resistance, made radiant by holiness.

They are the ones who did not lose their identity in Babylon. They carry scars, but not shame. They have war stories, but no retreat. Revelation 19:7 declares, *"The marriage of the Lamb has come, and His bride has made herself ready."* The remnant doesn't wait to be rescued - they rise to be refined. Their garments are washed in worship. Their eyes are set on the King. And their hearts burn with the eternal gospel, alive with heaven's thunder and urgency.

Jesus is coming for a church that has been through the fire, a church without spot, wrinkle, or blemish. Not a wrinkled teenage bride, but a full-grown woman. They are the ones who cry out in the wilderness, who discern the season, who have made themselves ready. Their voice shakes the systems of man. They are the ones who still pray, still fast, still confront demons. They are not deceived by the sound of Babylon; they are tuned to the frequency of the King.

As Revelation 14:4 says, *"These are the ones who follow the Lamb wherever He goes."* Their allegiance is to the King and His government, not religious tradition. Joel 2:12-13 reminds us that God honors the inward tearing of the heart over the outward display. The remnant does not perform for crowds - they respond to the King.

When the Crowd Leaves, the Called Remain

Remnants are revealed when crowds walk away. They emerge when popularity fades, when convenience no longer cushions commitment. Don't unsettle your soul by saying it will be over at any moment. He's not coming until the job is done. The remnant understands this. They are not escapists. They are laborers. They do not pray for rapture; they pray for harvest. They do not flee the battle; they run into it with the blood-stained banner of the King.

Hear this cry, "Unpack your rapture bag! He's not coming till we do the job He sent us to do." This isn't a time to escape; it's a time to establish. A time to build altars, disciple nations, and carry the gospel of the Kingdom until cities are shaken. The city can be healed if the church can be healed. They know this is not a rehearsal - it's Kingdom revolution.

Many started this journey, but few stayed. The ones who remain are not always the most gifted, but they are the most grounded. Their staying power is their anointing. Their refusal to bend is their mantle. They have been sifted and found faithful. They were not plucked from the fire to be spectators, but to be standard-bearers. The remnant rises when the crowd thins.

Jesus Himself confronted this in John 6:66-69, when many disciples turned away. But Peter, a remnant voice, declared, *"Lord, to whom shall we go? You have the words of eternal life."* The remnant doesn't flinch when the message gets hard - they dig deeper.

End-Time Boldness

These are not timid believers. They are not Sunday-only Christians with edited convictions. The remnant is fierce. They are those of whom the world is not worthy (Hebrews 11:38). They stand when others bow. They shout when others whisper. They offend religious systems with unapologetic truth. "You cannot break agreement with Babylon while still seeking its approval... this is the war between boldness and shame."

They are the Davids who run toward Goliath. The Esthers who approach the king uninvited. The Peters who preach in the face of prison. Their courage is not personality; it is prophetic. They are bold because they have seen the King. And once you have seen the King, you lose the fear of men. They declare with fire: "I break agreement with every lie. I renounce the counterfeit and embrace the King."

When you align with the King, shame dies. Compromise dies. The opinions of man die. Because you've encountered the one thing that works every time - the eternal gospel, alive with heaven's thunder and urgency. Their boldness is the result of a broken agreement with Babylon. They have chosen fire over fame, truth over trend.

Their weapon is not their volume - it is their purity. They are unmoved by trends because they are anchored in truth. Revelation 12:11 says, *"They overcame him by the blood of the Lamb and the word of their testimony, and they loved not their lives unto death."* That's the definition of remnant boldness.

Characteristics of the Remnant Church

The remnant church is not known for its size, but for its surrender. It may not have the best production, but it has the presence. It may not fill arenas, but it fills altars. It casts out demons. It heals the sick. It preaches repentance. It carries the eternal gospel, alive with heaven's thunder and urgency of the glorious Kingdom of unshakable authority and peace.

This church is multiethnic, multigenerational, and mission-minded. It transcends denominational tags. It values purity over polish. It chooses holiness over hype. It makes disciples, not fans. It trains warriors, not watchers. It sends, equips, delivers, and advances.

The remnant church is marked by:
- A clear distinction between the gospel of salvation and the gospel of the Kingdom.
- Uncompromising proclamation of truth, even when it costs.
- Worship that enthrones God, not entertains men.
- Prophetic intercession that births movements.
- A hunger for holiness that rejects cultural conformity.

Listen to this roar, "You were not born to repeat cycles. You were born to reign." And reign begins in the posture of surrender. The remnant church carries the fragrance of Christ (2 Corinthians 2:15), the authority of the cross, and the fire of heaven. *"I'm not ashamed of the eternal gospel, alive with heaven's thunder and urgency."* That is not just a confession. It is a war cry.

They are churches like Antioch - fasting, praying, sending. They are homes filled with power, not pretense. They do not negotiate with demons. They do not apologize for deliverance. They preach like eternity is near because it is.

The Rise Begins Now

This chapter is not just information - it is a roll call. The trumpet is sounding. Heaven is counting. Are you among the remnant? Have you come out from Babylon? Have you shaken the dust of compromise from your feet? Have you chosen fire over comfort? This is the moment where the called rise. The fainthearted fall back. And the remnant takes its place.

So cry aloud:

I am not ashamed of the eternal gospel, alive with heaven's thunder and urgency of the glorious Kingdom of unshakable authority and peace.

Let the world mock. Let religion resist. Let Babylon rage. But let the remnant rise.

Scripture References:

- Isaiah 1:9
- Revelation 19:7
- Romans 1:16
- Hebrews 11:38
- Matthew 6:33
- Galatians 1:8-9
- Revelation 18:4
- Romans 11:5
- 2 Timothy 1:7
- Acts 4:29-31
- John 6:66-69
- Luke 9:62

- Matthew 24:13
- 2 Corinthians 2:15
- 1 Peter 2:9
- Joel 2:12-13
- Revelation 14:4
- Judges 7:7
- Romans 11:4
- Philippians 1:29
- 2 Timothy 4:2-5
- Luke 6:26
- Ephesians 6:19-20
- Acts 13:2-3
- 2 Corinthians 6:17
- Ephesians 5:27
- Matthew 16:18
- Luke 10:19
- Galatians 5:1

Chapter Ten

Repentance – The Forgotten Door

What Repentance Really Means (Acts 3:19)

Repentance has been domesticated. We've reduced it to a polite apology or a momentary tear. But heaven sees repentance as the doorway - the sacred gate through which transformation rushes in like a flood. Acts 3:19 thunders the call: *"Repent therefore, and turn back, that your sins may be blotted out, that times of refreshing may come from the presence of the Lord."*

Repentance is not sorrow - it is surrender. It is not emotion - it is alignment. It does not begin with regret; it begins with revelation. That sudden, blinding realization: I have aligned with Babylon and not the King. It is the Aha moment that breaks the spell. It is the sudden clarity that everything you called freedom was actually chains. It is the thunderous shaking that says, This Gospel still works. But it will never bless what it came to dismantle.

You must reject every imitation. Every lukewarm imitation of Kingdom that avoids obedience, power, and holiness. True repentance is a violent confrontation with counterfeit Christianity - a declaration that the eternal Gospel, alive with heaven's thunder and urgency, is not merely a message of salvation, but of governmental realignment.

You cannot break agreement with Babylon while still seeking its approval. That is the essence of repentance. It is not just turning 'from' something - it is turning 'toward' Someone. A King. A Government. A Voice. To repent is to renounce the throne of self and rejoin the throne of God. It is not just a mental change; it is a complete regime change. It is to declare with your soul: The throne of my life is no longer vacant. It belongs to the King of Glory.

Listen to the warning, The Gospel doesn't just offer comfort - it commands transformation. Repentance, then, is Heaven's governmental summons to step out of deception and into dominion. This is echoed in Ezekiel 18:30: *"Repent, and turn yourselves from all your transgressions; so iniquity shall not be your ruin."* God is not calling you back to guilt - He's calling you forward into glory.

Turning from Dead Works

Dead works are not always evil works - they are just unauthorized. They are the acts done without intimacy, service without surrender, performance without presence. Hebrews 6:1 urges us to move beyond *"repentance from dead works,"* meaning that real repentance must divorce us from every false source of righteousness.

You can fast and still be rebellious. You can tithe and still be prideful. You can serve and still be self-righteous. Repentance calls out the imposter and demands eviction. "You don't break agreement with Babylon by simply changing behavior. You break it by changing how you respond."

Babylon trains you to perform. The Kingdom demands your posture. Repentance is not about quitting sin - it's about quitting self-rule. It is spiritual divorce from a system that told you it loved you but kept you enslaved. It's rejecting the religion that taught you how to act like a Christian without being transformed into a son. When you repent, you are not just confessing sin - you are announcing a transfer of power.

This cuts deep: "You were not called to manage dysfunction - you were called to crucify it." Repentance is not behavior modification - it is regime overthrow. It tears down the counterfeit kingdom and installs the rule of Christ. Isaiah 1:16-17 declares, *"Wash yourselves; make yourselves clean; remove the evil of your deeds from before My eyes; cease to do evil, learn to do good."*

This is why the Gospel Paul preached wasn't a comfort blanket - it was a Kingdom. "*I am not ashamed of the Gospel, for it is the power of God unto salvation*" (Romans 1:16). And that power confronts dead religion, uproots toxic tradition, and declares war on every altar built to self.

From Tears to Transformation

Tears are not repentance. Transformation is. You can cry over the consequences of sin and still be bound to its voice. True repentance produces fruit. As John the Baptist declared, "*Bear fruit in keeping with repentance*" (Matthew 3:8).

The problem in modern Christianity is we have made repentance a one-time event instead of a daily rhythm. We apologize, we feel bad, and then we return to the very thing that wounded us. That is not repentance - that is regret.

You cannot crucify what you keep excusing. And you cannot renounce what you're still feeding. Repentance cuts ties. It slams doors. It draws lines in the sand and says, "I will not go back." It severs emotional contracts. It breaks silent agreements made in pain. It doesn't just say sorry - it says, "never again."

It's a war. Not with people, but with patterns. Not with others, but with every internal agreement that allowed Babylon to whisper and remain. Repentance is the sword that severs those soul ties. It is the sledgehammer that crushes the altar of compromise. You cannot cast out what you keep inviting in.

Every outburst, every secret habit, every emotional idol - these are not random failures. They are roots of agreement still alive in the soul. True repentance yanks out those roots and burns them on the altar. 2 Corinthians 7:10 reminds us, "*Godly sorrow brings repentance that leads to salvation and leaves no regret, but worldly sorrow brings death.*"

Repentance does not preserve your reputation - it restores your authority. It doesn't make you look good - it makes you clean. And clean vessels carry Kingdom fire.

The Revival of Repentance

God is reintroducing repentance to His people - not as punishment, but as permission. The permission to be free. The permission to be whole. The permission to walk in authority without the stench of compromise. Repentance is not God shaming you - it's God summoning you.

This is the hour to break every lingering agreement with Babylon. Not by hype. Not by shame. But by Holy surrender. You were not born to repeat cycles. You were born to reign.

Repentance is the trumpet that announces: The King has come. And I yield to His reign. It is the voice that echoes through every false system and declares, Babylon must fall in me, so the Kingdom can rise.

Let the remnant cry aloud again: "I break agreement with Babylon. I renounce the lies. I sever every soul tie to my past. I align with the voice of the King. I repent. I turn. I rise."

This is not just a chapter. It is a call. A call to the altar. A call to the mirror. A call to the battlefield. Because repentance is the forgotten door. And behind that door is everything you've been praying for. As Revelation 3:19 says, *"Those whom I love I rebuke and discipline. So be earnest and repent."*

Repent, therefore, and turn to God, that your sins may be blotted out, and that times of refreshing may come from the presence of the Lord. (Acts 3:19)

Let the fire fall. Let shame break. Let truth speak. Let repentance roar. And let the Kingdom rise.

Scripture References:

- Acts 3:19
- Ezekiel 18:30
- Hebrews 6:1
- Isaiah 1:16-17
- Romans 1:16
- Matthew 3:8
- 2 Corinthians 7:10
- 1 Corinthians 15:31
- 2 Corinthians 10:5
- Psalm 139:23-24
- Revelation 3:19

Chapter Eleven

Truth That Divides

A Sword, Not a Feather

From the beginning, truth was never meant to pacify. It was meant to pierce. When Jesus declared, *"Do not think that I came to bring peace on earth. I did not come to bring peace but a sword"* (Matthew 10:34), He wasn't speaking metaphorically. He was drawing a line in the spirit. The eternal gospel, alive with heaven's thunder and urgency, doesn't stroke egos or preserve false peace - it divides. It separates light from darkness, allegiance from apathy, and Kingdom sons from Babylon's slaves. Babylon traffics in mixture. But the Kingdom calls for clarity.

Truth doesn't stroke dysfunction. It severs it. And that severing is not always welcomed. You must be willing to endure the sword if you want to carry the glory. There is no such thing as painless purification. The gospel of the Kingdom does not come to negotiate with your brokenness. It comes to kill what God never planted. This chapter is a declaration: Truth does not bring unity until it first brings division.

The prophet Jeremiah spoke of this as a fire and a hammer: *"Is not My word like a fire? says the LORD, and like a hammer that breaks the rock in pieces?"* (Jeremiah 23:29). Fire consumes what cannot remain. The hammer shatters what refuses to bow. We do not advance the Kingdom by trimming the truth. We advance it by releasing the full weight of the Word without shame.

The gospel that offends will always be the gospel that transforms. This is not a message of gentle adjustments but divine overhaul. The line is being drawn. What you tolerate will define you.

Why the Real Gospel Offends (Luke 12:51)

Jesus Himself said, *"Do you think I came to bring peace on earth? No, I tell you, but division"* (Luke 12:51). The real gospel is offensive because it reveals. It doesn't whisper; it roars. It doesn't flatter; it confronts. And confrontation is the path to transformation. When the eternal gospel, alive with heaven's thunder and urgency, is preached, it disrupts false loyalties and exposes hidden idols. It forces decisions. It dismantles neutrality.

Babylon wants your silence. Babylon is comfortable with a gospel that stays soft, that comforts dysfunction and avoids confrontation. But this gospel - this real gospel - requires repentance, not applause. It commands you to die to self, not discover yourself. We are not called to comfort, we are called to fire. We have become ashamed of the eternal gospel, alive with heaven's thunder and urgency... and that's why we're not having the effects of the gospel! Shame neuters truth. Silence delays deliverance. The gospel does not just offend - it divides.

You don't need another encouraging message. You need an encounter with the message that rearranges your entire worldview. This is the kind of gospel that turns tables in temples and exposes the fraud of spiritual apathy.

Paul asked in Galatians 4:16, "*Have I therefore become your enemy because I tell you the truth?*" The answer in every generation is often yes. Truth unmasks false comfort and exposes counterfeit covenants. You cannot preach deliverance while keeping people comfortable in their chains.

Division Is a Sign of God's Move

We have confused unity with approval. But the truth of the gospel exposes the counterfeit. Wherever the Kingdom moves, division occurs. That's not dysfunction - that's divine disruption. When Jesus walked into the temple, He didn't blend in. He flipped tables. When Paul preached in synagogues, cities rioted. That's what real truth does.

God will remove what threatens your breakthrough. He will strip away what partners with Babylon.

Division is not the problem. It's proof. It reveals who is surrendered and who is seduced. This is why Luke 12:51 is not a contradiction of the Prince of Peace. It is confirmation that peace is a byproduct of surrendered hearts, not compromised truth.

Amos 3:3 asks, "*Can two walk together, unless they are agreed?*" The answer is no. Division comes to distinguish between those aligned with the throne and those bowing to idols. This is the mercy of God - that He would separate us to sanctify us.

The real gospel offends until it transforms. It breaks before it builds. We must understand that when division comes through truth, it is a scalpel in the hand of a skilled surgeon. Not to destroy - but to deliver.

When the gospel is preached, families divide. Churches split. Friendships collapse. Why? Because the spirit of Babylon cannot coexist with the reign of Christ. The sword of the Spirit doesn't make suggestions. It makes war.

False Unity vs. Kingdom Unity

Not all unity is holy. There is a unity that protects idols. A unity that defends sin. A unity that says, "Let's not rock the boat." But Kingdom unity is forged in fire. It is alignment with truth, not alignment with culture. Jesus prayed, *"Sanctify them by Your truth. Your word is truth"* (John 17:17). That's the foundation of real unity.

You can't anoint Babylon. You must leave it.

False unity bows to popularity. Kingdom unity bows to the King. Babylon says, "Don't judge."

Zion says, "Righteous judgment restores order." Babylon creates churches filled with silent agreements. Zion builds movements born in holy disruption. And if your unity is more important than your purity, then your loyalty is still to Babylon.

You were not born to repeat cycles. You were born to reign. And reign begins at the altar, where you call it what God calls it - and walk out free. There is no unity without purity, and no purity without separation.

"*Now I beseech you, brethren, mark them which cause divisions and offenses contrary to the doctrine which ye have learned; and avoid them*" (Romans 16:17). This is not a call to reject people, but to guard the purity of the Word. The Church cannot unite around mixture. It must unite around Majesty.

How to Stand Firm in the Fire

You will be tested. When the gospel offends your friends, your family, your church - will you still preach it? When the pressure mounts, and culture demands silence, will you declare it louder? The mark of the remnant is not perfection - it's perseverance.

Standing firm means declaring like Paul: *"I am not ashamed of the eternal gospel, alive with heaven's thunder and urgency of Jesus Christ."* (Romans 1:16)

We are warned: The moment you are ashamed, it starts your descent into mediocracy and a suffocating darkness that veils hearts. Shame is a snare. But boldness is a weapon. When something breaks in you, and you are no longer ashamed, the enemy loses jurisdiction over your voice.

This gospel still delivers addicts, silences demons, mends marriages, restores broken minds. It's not an old truth. It's an eternal one. That's why the fight for your voice is fierce - because hell fears what you will declare once unashamed.

You do not need consensus to stand. You need conviction. Elijah stood alone on Mount Carmel and called down fire. Daniel stood alone in Babylon and refused to bow. You will not survive these days by trying to fit in. You will only thrive by standing out.

Ephesians 6:13 says, "*Therefore take up the whole armor of God, that you may be able to withstand in the evil day, and having done all, to stand.*" Standing is not passive. It is prophetic resistance. When you stand, heaven records your loyalty.

Call to Boldness and Final Declarations

Truth is not gentle. It is glorious. It is a flame that refines, a hammer that breaks, a sword that divides. And in this hour, God is calling for those who will not flinch. Who will not apologize for holiness. Who will not dilute the fire to gain followers.

Declare this now:

"I break agreement with false peace. I break agreement with cultural compromise. I align with the eternal gospel, alive with heaven's thunder and urgency of the glorious Kingdom of unshakable authority and peace!"

"I will not be ashamed. I will not be silent. I will not bow to Babylon. I will stand. I will speak. I will burn with truth."

Let the dividing sword do its work. Let every counterfeit connection be severed. Let every illusion of unity be exposed. And let the remnant rise. Bold. Unashamed. On fire.

Every time you preach the Kingdom, hell shakes and heaven stands. You are not a motivational speaker. You are a royal ambassador. The gospel you carry is not opinion - it is ordinance.

For the Kingdom is not for the comfortable. It is for the courageous. And in the end, only truth will remain.

Scripture References:
- Matthew 10:34
- Luke 12:51
- Romans 1:16
- Galatians 4:16
- Amos 3:3
- John 17:17
- Romans 16:17
- Jeremiah 23:29
- Ephesians 6:13

Chapter Twelve

When Identity Is Rebuilt

Reconstructing the Ruins

There is a cry deep within the human soul, echoing through the corridors of time, a desperate question: *Who am I?* Since the fall in Eden, mankind has suffered a rupture in identity. The serpent did not just tempt Eve to eat. He tempted her to forget who she was. Babylon exploits this wound by offering counterfeit identities - based on trauma, titles, performance, or pain. But Heaven is sounding a different call: Come back to who you really are.

In the ashes of your false self, God is ready to rebuild. The same hands that formed Adam from dust now reach into your ruin and whisper again: *You are Mine.* Your identity was never meant to be rooted in behavior, labels, or comparison. It was meant to be anchored in sonship. And until that identity is restored, shame will always have jurisdiction.

You were never called to earn your place - you were called to receive it. Babylon told you to strive. The Kingdom says, "Rest in who I've made you to be." This chapter is a call to tear down every false construct and let the Father rebuild what hell tried to bury.

The Gospel of the Kingdom is not just about what God gives - it's about what He requires. It has a positive side and a negative side. Like a battery, it carries both the power to spark life and the shock of conviction. When the gospel of identity is preached, it doesn't only affirm - it confronts. It exposes the orphan system and demands sonship alignment.

Isaiah 58:12 declares, *"Those from among you shall build the old waste places; you shall raise up the foundations of many generations."* You are not being rebuilt as who you were - you are being rebuilt as who you were always meant to be.

The restoration of identity is not a rehabilitation - it is a resurrection. The same power that raised Jesus from the grave (Romans 8:11) is the same power now reconstructing the true you.

From Orphan to Sonship

You can sit in church your entire life and still live as an orphan. Orphanhood is not the absence of community - it's the absence of belonging. It's the echo of rejection that says, "You don't fit. You're not enough." But the Gospel comes to confront the orphan spirit with a Father's voice.

The Gospel doesn't just offer comfort - it commands transformation. And only when we yield fully can we walk freely. Transformation begins when you stop performing for love and start abiding in it. You are not tolerated - you are treasured.

Jesus didn't just come to save sinners - He came to restore sons. Romans 8:15 says, *"For you did not receive the spirit of bondage again to fear, but you received the Spirit of adoption by whom we cry out, 'Abba, Father.'"* The orphan cries for validation. The son rests in revelation. Your cry has changed.

John 1:12 affirms this transformation: *"But to all who did receive Him, to those who believed in His name, He gave the right to become children of God."* This is not mere belief - it's a divine legal adoption. It's the reversal of the rejection cycle.

Psalm 68:6 reminds us: *"God sets the solitary in families; He brings out those who are bound into prosperity."* You are not left alone in isolation - you are placed in belonging.

Deuteronomy 14:1 proclaims, *"You are the children of the Lord your God..."* This is not figurative language - it is a covenant declaration.

You don't need a new revelation - you need divine submission. You don't need a fresh word - you need to obey the last word. And the last word was this: "You are Mine."

You are no longer a beggar hoping for crumbs. You are a son seated at the table, with access to the King's authority and inheritance. Your past no longer defines your place. The blood has sealed your belonging.

Knowing Whose You Are

Before you can declare who you are, you must first know whose you are. Ownership defines identity. And in the Kingdom, identity begins in the presence of the King. You are not your past. You are not your pain. You are not what was done to you. You are His.

Your story is not your trauma. Your destiny is not your dysfunction. You are not shaped by who left or who failed you - but by the God who stayed.

The cross didn't just forgive you - it redefined you. *"Therefore, if anyone is in Christ, he is a new creation..."* (2 Corinthians 5:17). You are not a repaired version of your past - you are a new creation with a new name.

Ephesians 1:5 echoes this: *"He predestined us for adoption to sonship through Jesus Christ, in accordance with His pleasure and will."* God didn't save you reluctantly. He did it joyfully. He chose you before the foundations of the earth.

1 John 3:1 proclaims: *"Behold what manner of love the Father has bestowed on us, that we should be called children of God!"* Heaven's declaration trumps every earthly label.

Isaiah 43:1 says, *"Fear not, for I have redeemed you; I have called you by your name; you are Mine."* That is ownership. That is identity.

The Kingdom Gospel doesn't just rearrange your schedule - it rearranges your soul. And when your soul comes into alignment, every false identity is evicted.

When God names you, shame has no vote. When Heaven marks you, Babylon's labels lose their grip. The Kingdom is not a title you wear - it's a bloodline you belong to. And the King does not forget His own.

Authority Comes from Identity

You cannot walk in Kingdom authority if you are still questioning your legitimacy. Authority flows from alignment, and alignment begins in identity. Hell is not afraid of gifted people - it's terrified of those who know who they are.

Jesus didn't launch His ministry until He heard the Father say, *"This is My beloved Son, in whom I am well pleased"* (Matthew 3:17). That was not information. It was identity activation. And only after that moment did Jesus confront Satan in the wilderness.

You don't need a fresh word - you need to obey the last word. What was the last word the Father said to you? That's the anchor of your authority.

Luke 10:19 declares: *"Behold, I give you authority... over all the power of the enemy, and nothing shall by any means hurt you."* But that authority is only activated by identity. Orphans perform for access. Sons operate from it.

Proverbs 28:1 declares: *"The wicked flee when no one pursues, but the righteous are bold as a lion."* Your identity breeds your boldness.

1 Peter 2:9 confirms: *"But you are a chosen generation, a royal priesthood, a Holy nation, His own special people..."* That's not motivational speech - it's a spiritual designation.

Until you settle your identity, you will negotiate your calling. You'll seek affirmation from crowds instead of confirmation from the throne. But when you know who you are, the fear of man breaks. The confusion lifts. And demons start retreating.

The Gospel still works. It delivers addicts, silences demons, mends marriages, and restores broken minds. It's not an old truth. It's an eternal one.

Shame Breaks Where Sonship Rules

Shame is not just an emotion. It's a prison. It keeps you performing, pretending, and hiding. But shame cannot coexist with sonship. Where the Spirit of adoption is received, the weight of shame is shattered.

The reason we're so passive in the pulpit is because we've trained ourselves to protect people's feelings more than protect their destinies. But the real Gospel doesn't pat your head - it resets your heart.

You are not what happened to you. You are what Heaven calls you. Isaiah 61:7 declares, *"Instead of your shame you shall have double honor..."* That is not poetic - it's prophetic. The places where shame once ruled are now altars of restoration.

Galatians 4:6 says, *"Because you are sons, God sent the Spirit of His Son into our hearts, the Spirit who calls out, 'Abba, Father.'"* This is the cry of a rebuilt identity. Not one of fear - but one of familiarity with the Father.

Psalm 34:5 says, *"They looked to Him and were radiant, and their faces were not ashamed."* When God restores identity, shame has no legal ground to remain.

Isaiah 50:7 declares, *"For the Lord God will help me; therefore I will not be disgraced; therefore I have set my face like a flint..."* That is the posture of a son who knows his identity.

Warning: You cannot walk in Kingdom authority if you still live under Babylon's permission. To break shame, you must renounce Babylon's verdict and receive the King's decree.

Let the voice of the Father silence every whisper of the accuser. Let your name echo in Zion, not Babylon. And let the Kingdom rise in you - not as a theology, but as an identity. Because when identity is rebuilt, shame dies, authority rises, and sons return home.

Scripture References:

- Romans 8:11
- Romans 8:15
- John 1:12
- 2 Corinthians 5:17
- Matthew 3:17
- Isaiah 61:7
- Luke 10:19
- Galatians 4:6
- Ephesians 1:5
- 1 John 3:1

- John 15:15
- Luke 15:20-24
- Isaiah 58:12
- Psalm 68:6
- Proverbs 28:1

- Psalm 34:5
- Deuteronomy 14:1
- Isaiah 43:1
- 1 Peter 2:9
- Isaiah 50:7

Chapter Thirteen

Walking in Kingdom Authority

Introduction: The Kingdom Is Within You

The glorious Kingdom of unshakable authority and peace is not coming - it's already here. It's encoded in your design, woven into your nature by divine intent. When God breathed into Adam, He wasn't just giving breath; He was imparting government. Genesis 1:28 thunders with Holy mandate: *"Be fruitful, and multiply, and replenish the earth, and subdue it: and have dominion."* Dominion is not a gift - it's your nature. You were born to govern.

Luke 17:21 is not a metaphor. It's an unveiling. Jesus declared, "*The Kingdom of God is within you.*" That statement dismantles every powerless theology. It shatters religious systems that claim authority is reserved for the few, and it rips the veil that tradition has sewn over the eyes of God's people. The throne is not in the clouds - it's in you. The glorious Kingdom of unshakable authority and peace of God is written in your nature.

We have not preached the Gospel of the Kingdom - we have preached the gospel of the church. And the church is not the Kingdom. It is the embassy. It represents, but it does not replace. Just like the U.S. Embassy is not the United States but a representation of it, you are the representative of Heaven on earth. You don't wait for dominion; you awaken to it. The Spirit is saying: "Rise and reign." You were born for fire, not form. You were designed for authority, not attendance. You were not built to sit silently in pews but to roar in the streets with divine order and righteous fire. The Kingdom is not hidden in the heavens - it is crying to be revealed in you. Romans 8:19 reveals the cry: *"For the earnest expectation of the creation eagerly waits for the revealing of the sons of God."* The earth is waiting for you to rise.

Not Just Saved - Sent

Salvation was not your conclusion - it was your commissioning. It was never meant to be a passive escape plan but a divine deployment. Salvation is not a pause - it's a propulsion. When the blood touched your spirit, you weren't just forgiven - you were enlisted. Forgiveness removed the weight of sin, but commissioning imparted the weight of glory. God didn't clean you up just so you could sit down - He filled you up so you could be sent out.

Jesus said in John 20:21, "As the Father has sent Me, I also send you." That's not symbolic. It is your Kingdom assignment. You are Heaven's representative on earth. You are not merely a convert - you are a catalyst. The moment redemption touched your life, you became dangerous to darkness. Acts 1:8 confirms it:

"But you shall receive power when the Holy Spirit has come upon you; and you shall be witnesses to Me..."

We still have a right to preach the Gospel of the Kingdom. And I'm not going to back up. If you've been touched by the coal of the altar, your lips are now weapons of mass deliverance. If your mouth has been redeemed, your voice is now a trumpet. Your silence can become sin when your call is to speak. This Gospel is not therapy - it is fire. Not opinion, but ordinance. Not comfort, but commission. And the enemy fears your revelation of who you are.

So declare it: "I am not ashamed of the Gospel of the Kingdom. I was not just saved to survive. I was saved to subdue. I carry divine authority to shift atmospheres, break chains, and heal the sick." Say it again until your identity aligns with Heaven's intention.

Power Over Darkness

Darkness is not metaphorical - it's militant. It doesn't ask permission. It occupies unless confronted. That's why Jesus didn't negotiate with demons - He cast them out. Mark 1:27 says, *"With authority He commands even the unclean spirits, and they obey Him."* That same authority is in you. But authority only flows through alignment.

James 4:7 reveals the formula: *"Submit yourselves therefore to God. Resist the devil, and he will flee from you."* Submission is not weakness. It is warfare. Hell fears a submitted believer more than a shouting one. Because alignment with the King releases jurisdiction.

You cannot deliver this city unless you preach what He preached. What did Jesus preach? The Kingdom. He didn't preach a gospel of comfort. He preached a Gospel that cast out, called out, and changed everything. He disrupted atmospheres. He upset the religious order. He walked into synagogues and exposed systems. That same disruptive, confrontational fire now lives in you.

Revelation 12:11 testifies: "*They overcame him by the blood of the Lamb, and by the word of their testimony.*" Your testimony is not just your story - it is your sword. Every time you speak what God did, you issue a decree that dismantles demonic contracts. Your voice, soaked in blood and backed by Heaven, silences hell.

So rise and say it: "I am not ashamed of deliverance. I'm not ashamed of tongues. I'm not ashamed of healing. I am not ashamed of the eternal Gospel, alive with heaven's thunder and urgency of Jesus Christ! I speak and darkness flees. I declare and demons tremble."

The Apostolic Mandate of Every Believer

Apostolic is not a title - it's a trajectory. It means "sent with government." Every believer carries this mandate. You don't need a pulpit to be apostolic - you need obedience. Jeremiah 1:10

declares, *"See, I have this day set you over the nations and over the kingdoms, to root out and to pull down, to destroy and to throw down, to build and to plant."*

Listen to this rebuke if you desire a platform without price: You mean you want to work in the embassy? You want the position, but do you want the fire? True apostolic believers don't chase microphones. They build altars. They don't mimic success. They manifest the Kingdom. They don't seek popularity - they seek impact. And they don't ask, "Will this make me famous?" They ask, "Will this make Him known?"

Matthew 16:19 confirms our authority: "*I will give you the keys of the Kingdom... whatever you bind on earth will be bound in Heaven...*" Keys aren't given to spectators - they're given to stewards. The fire of governance is falling again, and the Spirit is searching for builders. Isaiah 58:12 echoes this mandate: "*And they that shall be of thee shall build the old waste places...*"

So rise and declare: "I am a Kingdom legislator. I carry the fire to uproot and rebuild. I do not need permission to obey. I have been sent. I will root out confusion, cast down compromise, and plant righteousness."

You Are Heaven's Embassy

The church is not the Kingdom - it's the embassy. You are not just a believer. You are jurisdiction. Philippians 3:20 reminds us: *"Our citizenship is in Heaven."* And 2 Corinthians 5:20 makes it clear: *"We are ambassadors for Christ..."*

The church is the embassy. It's not the Kingdom, but it represents it. That means when you show up, the government of God arrives. Your prayers are decrees. Your worship is warfare. Your presence is policy.

You don't carry opinions - you carry authority. You are not a weak voice in a loud world - you are a governing voice in a broken system. You carry the full weight of Heaven wherever you go. When you speak, devils lose jurisdiction. When you praise, prison doors open. When you intercede, policies in the spirit realm are written.

Job 22:28 prophesies: *"You will also declare a thing, and it will be established for you; so light will shine on your ways."* That's jurisdiction. That's lawmaking in the spirit.

So declare boldly: "I am Heaven's embassy. I do not walk in fear. I legislate peace. I declare healing. I release deliverance. I represent the King. My house is an embassy. My family is a stronghold. My city is under my intercession."

Reclaiming the Forgotten Authority

Somewhere between tradition and religion, we forgot who we were. We traded boldness for branding. We chose titles over territory. But the trumpet is sounding again. The King is calling

His ambassadors to rise. Not in theory, but in truth. Not with noise, but with authority.

Romans 8:37 declares: "*Yet in all these things we are more than conquerors through Him who loved us.*" We are not survivors - we are enforcers. And now, the Spirit is commissioning a remnant to walk in the authority of the eternal Gospel, alive with heaven's thunder and urgency.

You cannot walk in Kingdom authority if you still live under Babylon's permission. So shake off every religious muzzle. Break agreement with fear. Rise in the fire of your calling. Step out of form and into fire. Leave religious survival and enter prophetic dominion.

Declare it with thunder: "I walk in power. I walk in boldness. I carry the authority of the King. I will speak. I will heal. I will cast out. I will govern. I am not ashamed. This is not a rehearsal. This is Kingdom. And I have been sent."

Scripture References:

- Genesis 1:28
- Luke 17:21
- Romans 8:19
- John 20:21
- Acts 1:8
- Mark 1:27
- James 4:7
- Revelation 12:11
- Jeremiah 1:10
- Matthew 16:19
- Isaiah 58:12
- Philippians 3:20
- 2 Corinthians 5:20
- Job 22:28

Chapter Fourteen

Babylon Must Fall

Tearing Down Strongholds

From Eden to Egypt, from Babel to Babylon, the strongholds of rebellion have always carried one goal: to exalt man above God. Babylon, in every era, has been the exaltation of human pride against divine purpose. And now, in this age of compromise and cultural confusion, Babylon breathes again. Not as a city, but as a system - a seductive structure designed to make the Church irrelevant, quiet, and ashamed.

But let it be declared: Babylon must fall.

Tearing down strongholds is not an emotional moment; it is a prophetic mandate. Paul wrote in 2 Corinthians 10:4-5, "*For the weapons of our warfare are not carnal but mighty through God to the pulling down of strongholds; casting down imaginations, and every high thing that exalteth itself against the knowledge of God.*" This is war. And Babylon is not just a name - it is a high thing. It is a system built on imagination, idolatry, and iniquity. And it must be cast down.

Babylon thrives on unchallenged lies. It survives on unspoken agreements. Warning: You cannot cast out Babylon with fleshly wisdom. You cannot negotiate with the system that crucified your King. You must discern it, confront it, and walk out of it. The Spirit of Babylon is embedded in belief systems, pulpits without power, and gospels that promote comfort over transformation. And the longer we tolerate it, the deeper its roots grow.

Babylon is a spirit of substitution. It offers religion without relationship, comfort without consecration, crowds without covenant. And until those spiritual contracts are broken, Babylon still reigns within. This is why every stronghold must be unseated not by intellect, but by obedience. When the fire of the Kingdom burns, it exposes every high place erected in defiance of God's government. And when we preach the eternal Gospel, alive with Heaven's thunder and urgency of the glorious Kingdom of unshakable authority and peace, strongholds shake. Demons tremble. Confusion clears.

Further, Ephesians 6:12 reminds us that "...*we wrestle not against flesh and blood, but against principalities and powers - spiritual hosts of wickedness...*" This means Babylon's power is not primarily human but demonic. It cannot be dismantled with carnal weapons, clever slogans, or strategic branding. It must be struck with truth, repentance, and the authority of Christ's name. Let every high thing fall, and let the King take His throne again.

Exiting Cultural Christianity

Cultural Christianity is Babylon in disguise. It sings songs of freedom while remaining shackled to tradition. It applauds sermons it never applies. It wears the cross as jewelry but refuses to carry it. It nods at holiness but never pursues it. It gives God lip service while serving Pharaoh in the heart. And we must exit this counterfeit if we are to enter the Kingdom.

Jesus said in Matthew 7:21, "*Not everyone who says to Me, 'Lord, Lord,' will enter the Kingdom of Heaven, but he who does the will of My Father.*" That statement wasn't aimed at pagans; it was a rebuke to the religious. The ones who had the language of the Kingdom but not the lifestyle. The ones who stayed in church but never came out of Babylon.

You don't need another encouraging message. You need an encounter with the message that rearranges your entire worldview. This is the demand of Kingdom truth. It doesn't negotiate; it demands. It doesn't whisper; it thunders.

You cannot walk in Kingdom authority if you still live under Babylon's permission. This is the danger of cultural Christianity - it trains people to coexist with bondage while calling it blessed. It teaches believers to polish their image while their altars remain broken. It equips them to fit in, not to stand out. It preaches a gospel that leaves you bound, comforts dysfunction, and rejects transformation.

Romans 12:2 urges, "*Do not conform to the pattern of this world, but be transformed by the renewing of your mind.*" Cultural Christianity conforms. Kingdom life transforms. Exiting cultural Christianity requires renewing the mind, crucifying the flesh, and submitting every ambition to the government of God.

To exit means more than leaving a church culture - it means burning the bridges to every religious substitute. It means choosing holiness over hype, obedience over opinions, and fire over form. As Paul declared, "*I am not ashamed of the Gospel of Christ*" (Romans 1:16).

You cannot cast out Babylon while sipping from her cup. You cannot sing Zion's songs while feeding Babylon's appetite. To exit cultural Christianity is to step into Holy distinction. To become a peculiar people again. A remnant people. A Kingdom people.

Calling the Church Out of Egypt

When God delivered Israel from Egypt, He didn't just bring them out of a place - He brought them out of a system. Egypt was a structure of control, manipulation, and fear. And even after Israel left physically, Egypt still echoed in their hearts. They longed for the leeks and the onions while forgetting the whip.

We preach grace but build like Pharaoh. We celebrate deliverance but function in slavery. This is the tragedy of a Church that has come out of sin but not out of bondage. We wear Kingdom garments, but operate in an Egyptian hierarchy. We sing of freedom, yet structure our ministries like prisons. We call it leadership, but Heaven calls it bondage.

Isaiah 52:11 declares, "*Depart! Depart! Go out from there! Touch no unclean thing! Come out from it and be pure, you who carry the articles of the LORD's house.*" Babylon's system of religious bondage must be rejected. We are not performers. We are priests. We do not exist for applause. We exist for glory.

Hebrews 3:16-19 reveals that those who left Egypt could not enter the promise because of unbelief. God is not just delivering people from sin - He's delivering them from systems of unbelief that mimic religious fervor but lack Kingdom fruit. You can sing about Canaan and die in the wilderness if your heart refuses the government of the King.

Stop asking God to bless what He came to dismantle. You can't anoint Babylon. You must leave it. You cannot enter Canaan while longing for Egypt. You cannot carry the ark while living in Pharaoh's courts. You must choose. Because when Babylon falls, only those aligned with Zion will stand. Hebrews 12:27 reminds us that everything that can be shaken will be shaken - so that what cannot be shaken may remain.

Babylon's Fall Is the Church's Rise

Revelation 18:2-4 is not poetic language. It is a prophetic summons: "*Fallen! Fallen is Babylon the Great!... Come out of her, My people, so that you will not share in her sins, so that you will not receive any of her plagues.*"

Babylon's fall is not just about judgment. It is about transition. As Babylon collapses, the Church must rise. Not a church of buildings and branding, but a remnant Church ablaze with holiness, filled with power, aligned with Heaven.

Babylon must fall in you before it can fall around you. It begins with internal altars being rebuilt, hidden idols being smashed, and personal repentance becoming public transformation. Babylon's fall is the alarm clock of the Spirit, awakening the bride to her real identity.

Let the Spirit of God rise in you now. Let shame be broken, truth be revealed, and Kingdom be established. This is not poetic imagery; it is Kingdom reality. We are stepping into the era of reformation. A shaking that will separate wheat from chaff. A moment where Sunday performances will be exposed, and only true Kingdom carriers will remain.

Joel 2:1 commands, "*Blow the trumpet in Zion, sound the alarm on My Holy hill.*" Babylon's fall is that trumpet. It is the call for priests to rise, prophets to weep between porch and altar, and saints to return to first love. The Church must not mourn Babylon's fall. We must celebrate it.

Because when Babylon falls, purity rises. When Babylon falls, boldness returns. When Babylon falls, the true sons and daughters of God begin to walk in power, truth, and unshakable authority.

So, stand tall, remnant. Refuse the compromise. Renounce the religion of Babylon. Walk out of her systems, her schedules, her seductions. Because as Babylon falls, the Church rises.

And this rising Church will not be ashamed. This rising Church will not apologize for power. This rising Church will cast out demons, raise the dead, disciple nations, and call cities into alignment with the glorious Kingdom of unshakable authority and peace.

Babylon must fall. And when it does, we will rise.

Scripture References:
- 2 Corinthians 10:4-5
- Matthew 7:21
- Romans 1:16
- Isaiah 52:11
- Revelation 18:2-4
- Hebrews 12:27
- Matthew 6:33
- Romans 14:17
- Ephesians 6:12
- Romans 12:2
- Hebrews 3:16-19
- Joel 2:1

Chapter Fifteen

The Return Home

The Prodigal Nation

The story of the prodigal son is more than a parable - it is a prophetic mirror held up to our generation. It is America. It is the modern Church. It is every believer who has known the voice of the Father yet traded His government for the glitter of Babylon. Luke 15:11-32 is not about a rebellious teenager; it is about a nation that took its anointing and invested it in rebellion. It is about pulpits that once thundered with truth but now tremble under the weight of public approval. It is about believers who left the glory of God for the comfort of culture.

We took the inheritance of grace, the mantle of authority, the Word of power, and spent it on dead movements and hollow performances. The Father gave us oil, and we used it to fuel our platforms. He gave us revelation, and we diluted it for popularity. He gave us truth, and we wrapped it in compromise. And now we sit among the pigs of political confusion, moral decay, and spiritual apathy.

Amos 8:11 declares, *"I will send a famine in the land, not a famine of bread or a thirst for water, but of hearing the words of the Lord."* That famine is here. We host worship nights without repentance.

We gather in conferences void of consecration. We post scriptures but silence the prophets. The result? A generation starved of Presence, stripped of power, and seduced by the husks of Babylon.

Yet even now, the Father's mercy reaches. You were not designed to remain in spiritual drought. You were created to burn with truth and reign with righteousness. The call is not to improvement - it is to resurrection. Return, not to a better version of religion, but to the fire of the King's throne room. Revelation 3:2-3 warns the slumbering church: "*Wake up! Strengthen what remains and is about to die... Remember, therefore, what you have received and heard; hold it fast, and repent.*"

The robe still fits, even after the mud. The ring still belongs, even after rebellion. The sandals still walk, even after wandering. The remnant is rising, not with polish, but with power. Not with fear, but with fire.

Come Out from Among Them

You cannot come home and stay in Babylon. The return demands a departure. 2 Corinthians 6:17 roars like a trumpet: "*Come out from among them and be separate, says the Lord. Do not touch what is unclean, and I will receive you.*" This is not a suggestion. It is a summons to war.

Babylon does not mind if you speak in tongues as long as you don't walk in holiness. It will let you sing as long as you don't separate. It offers church without change, identity without repentance, grace without government. But the Kingdom demands separation - not as a form of elitism, but as an act of allegiance.

"You cannot sip from the cup of the Lord and the cup of demons too." (1 Corinthians 10:21)

Every tolerated lie becomes a chain. Every compromised standard becomes a covenant with confusion. You cannot date Jesus and flirt with Jezebel. You cannot wear the Father's robe while sleeping in Babylon's bed. There is no dual citizenship in the Kingdom.

Shout with fire: "You can't partner with Babylon and pray like Zion. You must choose your allegiance. Either the Spirit of God governs you, or the system of Babylon does." James 4:4 thunders: "*Don't you know that friendship with the world is enmity with God?*"

The Kingdom is not looking for polite believers - it is summoning prophets. Every act of obedience unseats a principality. Every time you sever ties with compromise, you build an altar of truth. Like Elijah on Mount Carmel, it is time to repair the broken altar and call down the fire (1 Kings 18:30-39).

When you leave Babylon, you don't leave empty-handed. You leave with oil, fire, and a mandate. Exodus 3:10 was not just for Moses - it is for every voice called to deliver a people enslaved to Egypt's illusion. *"Come now, I will send you to Pharaoh that you may bring My people... out of Egypt."*

Restored Identity, Renewed Purpose

When the son returned, he didn't just get a hug. He received a robe, a ring, and sandals. Each carried prophetic weight. The robe spoke of identity. The ring represented restored authority. The sandals were proof of renewed purpose. Luke 15:22 is a divine template: *"Bring the best robe and put it on him. Put a ring on his finger and sandals on his feet."*

Isaiah 61:10 declares, *"He has clothed me with garments of salvation and arrayed me in a robe of his righteousness."* Romans 8:1 decrees, *"There is therefore now no condemnation for those who are in Christ Jesus."* That's not emotional comfort - that's judicial release.

The robe is not a costume. It's a covering. The ring is not jewelry. It's jurisdiction. The sandals are not accessories. They are an apostolic assignment.

Your pain did not disqualify you - it positioned you. Your wilderness was not punishment - it was preparation. Babylon may have tried to rename you, reframe you, and shame you - but the Father is here to restore what religion buried.

Isaiah 58:12 says, *"You shall be called the repairer of the breach, the restorer of streets to dwell in."* That is your mantle. Not a maintenance worker in church culture - but a reformer in Kingdom mandate. You were born to rebuild cities, restore altars, and revive generations. Your ring is not ornamental. It is governmental.

Joel 2:25 confirms the promise: "*I will restore to you the years that the swarming locust has eaten.*" Shame has no claim. Condemnation has no voice. The ring is your authority. The robe is your validation. The sandals are your re-commissioning.

Romans 8:19 confirms your assignment: *"For the creation waits with eager longing for the revealing of the sons of God."* The earth groans for your return. The nations wait for your voice. Babylon falls when your identity rises.

A Bride Made Ready for the King

Revelation 19:7 declares, "*Let us rejoice and be glad and give Him glory! For the wedding of the Lamb has come, and His bride has made herself ready.*" The Church is not a confused teenager. She is a grown woman, clothed in fire, marked by consecration.

Ephesians 5:27 says Jesus is coming for a glorious Church, without spot, wrinkle, or blemish. This is not legalism. This is Holy love. Babylon wears lipstick; Zion wears oil. Babylon hosts concerts; the Bride hosts glory. Babylon seduces. The Bride surrenders.

We are not dating the gospel. We are marrying the King. Let that burn into your bones. This is not the hour to dabble in devotion. It is the hour to burn with Holy jealousy. The Bride prepares by trimming her lamp, purifying her heart, and breaking all former engagements with compromise.

Matthew 25 warns us of the foolish virgins who had no oil. Let that not be said of you. Fill your lamp. Guard your fire. Worship like it matters. Pray like eternity is in the balance. Because it is.

This is not performance-driven Christianity. This is presence-driven allegiance. Only the pure in heart will see God (Matthew 5:8). Only the burning will be carried into the chamber. Only the consecrated will be commissioned in this next wave of revival.

I am not ashamed of deliverance. I am not ashamed of tongues. I am not ashamed of fire. I am not ashamed of the Gospel, alive with Heaven's thunder and urgency of the glorious Kingdom of unshakable authority and peace.

Let the Bride rise, not timid but tenacious. Let her cry be loud. Let her garments be white. Let her oil be overflowing. Let her love be fierce. Let her voice echo Revelation 22:17, "*The Spirit and the bride say, 'Come.'*"

Let her rise with the cry of Song of Songs 8:6: "*Set me as a seal upon your heart... for love is as strong as death, its jealousy unyielding as the grave. It burns like blazing fire, like a mighty flame.*"

Scripture References

- Luke 15:11-32
- Amos 8:11
- 2 Corinthians 6:17
- 1 Corinthians 10:21
- James 4:4
- 1 Kings 18:21, 30-39

- Isaiah 61:10
- Romans 8:1
- Romans 8:19
- Isaiah 58:12
- Revelation 19:7
- Ephesians 5:27
- Matthew 5:8
- Song of Songs 6:3
- Song of Songs 8:6
- Revelation 3:2-3
- Joel 2:25
- Matthew 25:1-13
- Revelation 22:17
- Exodus 3:10

Chapter Sixteen

The Final Separation

Delivered from Half-Kingdom Thinking

If it wasn't working, we might be ashamed. But it works. The eternal Gospel, alive with Heaven's thunder and urgency, works. And because it works, we will not apologize for it. We are here to deliver you from churchianity. We are here to deliver you from the diluted version of Christianity that masquerades as truth. We are here to tear down the altars of compromise and raise up a generation baptized in fire. This is the hour to expose the eternal Gospel, alive with Heaven's thunder and urgency of the glorious Kingdom of unshakable authority and peace. No more spiritual fog. No more lukewarm sermons. No more divided loyalties.

This is not just revival; it's regime change. Paul said in Galatians 1:8, *"But though we, or an angel from Heaven, preach any other gospel... let him be accursed."* Why? Because only the true Gospel carries fire that transforms. You can't dilute it and keep its power. The Gospel of the Kingdom is government. It doesn't just comfort - it conquers.

I have not come to echo the doctrines of men. I have come to shatter them.

I'm here to deliver you from the powerless gospel of mere escape - the diluted message that offers salvation without submission, forgiveness without government. That gospel may soothe the conscience, but it never transforms the soul. It leaves you saved but still enslaved. It tells you Jesus is your Savior, but never your King.

I have come to bring you the eternal gospel, alive with heaven's thunder and urgency - not just of salvation, but of government. A gospel where the cross is not just an altar of mercy, but a seat of dominion. A gospel where Jesus is not just the Lamb who saves, but the King who rules. This is the gospel of the Kingdom. This is the message that shakes hell and realigns the earth. And this is the only gospel that heaven endorses.

Don't Date Babylon

Lean in, especially you young warriors. How dare you date someone who doesn't tremble at the voice of the King? How dare you hold hands with someone who refuses to bow before the government of God? If they can't be loyal to Him, they won't be loyal to you. You're unequally yoked - you're on level 17, and they're stuck on level 2. You think it's harmless, but every compromise is a down payment on captivity. The very thing you were called to live for is the very thing they're resisting.

2 Corinthians 6:14 warns, *"Do not be unequally yoked together with unbelievers. For what fellowship has righteousness with lawlessness?"*

This is not about judgment - it's about destiny protection. Babylon's charm is deception dressed in affection. Don't fall for it. If they can't be true to the King, they won't be true to a creature. You're just not that cute.

Non-Negotiables of the Kingdom

The Kingdom has non-negotiables. There are patterns, principles, and divine blueprints that cannot be altered. The 10 Commandments are not ten suggestions. Every violation comes with consequence. Some sooner. Some later. But all of them will find you. You may hide your sin behind Christian lingo, but Heaven sees the truth. The spirit realm knows when you're playing church and when you're enforcing the government of God.

Jesus made it clear in Matthew 7:21, *"Not everyone who says to Me, 'Lord, Lord,' shall enter the Kingdom of Heaven, but he who does the will of My Father."* Obedience is not optional - it's proof of allegiance. You don't get to bend the rules and still expect the crown.

Every time you violate the Kingdom principles, you bring consequences to your life. They may be hidden for a while, but they will follow you.

The Roll Call of the Unashamed

Right now, in the spirit realm, angels are taking names. Not just of those who attend, but those who align. Not just those who shout, but those who submit. Not just those who believe, but those who burn. In this room and across this region, God is raising up a remnant that will not flinch, will not bow, and will not break under pressure. The fire is separating the pretenders from the possessors.

Romans 1:16 shouts, *"I am not ashamed of the Gospel of Christ, for it is the power of God unto salvation."* This is the dividing line: bold faith or hidden allegiance. Only the unashamed can carry the weight of awakening.

God has angels walking around taking people's names who made up their mind from this day forth: I will live and declare the eternal Gospel, alive with Heaven's thunder and urgency.

The Imitation Must Die

Let every counterfeit be exposed. Let every spirit of religion be silenced. Let every lukewarm gospel be stripped of its disguise. You were not made to flirt with Babylon. You were born to burn with Heaven. And some of you have been settling for a plan B relationship, a plan B calling, a plan B gospel. But God did not ordain substitutes. He ordained a Bride - spotless, full-grown, radiant.

Jesus said in Revelation 3:16, *"So then, because you are lukewarm, and neither cold nor hot, I will vomit you out of My mouth."* The true Gospel evokes a response - passion or persecution. But it never leaves you neutral.

"There is no other Kingdom to join. If you reject the message of the Kingdom, you reject the King who gave it."

Marked for Glory, Not for Compromise

You have been marked. And the devil knows it. That's why he has been trying to distract you with relationships that drain you, churches that tame you, and lies that shame you. But this is your awakening. This is your interruption. This is the final separation.

Jeremiah 1:5 says, *"Before I formed you in the womb I knew you; before you were born I sanctified you; I ordained you a prophet to the nations."* You are not random. You are marked. And the battle over your life is proof of your assignment.

God is about to bring a significant revival, but He must find people in whom something breaks. In front of your family. In front of your coworkers. You must say, 'I am not ashamed.'

The Echo of the King's Voice

He is calling your name. Not just for salvation, but for surrender. Not just for forgiveness, but for fire. He is not whispering religion. He is roaring dominion. And the moment you say yes - really yes - everything shifts. Your shame breaks. Your compromise dissolves. Your mouth becomes a trumpet. Your life becomes a decree. This is the sound of the final separation.

John 10:27 declares, *"My sheep hear My voice, and I know them, and they follow Me."* He is not silent. The King speaks with fire. But are you listening with surrender?

"When you align with the King, shame dies. Compromise dies. The opinions of man die. Because you've encountered the one thing that works every time - the eternal Gospel, alive with Heaven's thunder and urgency."

A Divine Encouragement and Final Warning

Listen, beloved. God will do everything He can to keep you out of hell. Because He knows how terrible it truly is. He knows how deep the torment, how eternal the separation, how final the judgment. So, He made it simple - so simple even a child could escape. The cross is your exit. The blood is your covering. The Word is your map. But hear this: while God longs to save you, He will not violate His own word.

"My covenant will I not break, nor alter the thing that is gone out of My lips." (Psalm 89:34)

He will not rewrite the scriptures to accommodate rebellion. He will not dilute truth to soothe your compromise. He will not bend His throne to fit your preferences. He is Holy. And He is just. But He is also kind beyond comprehension. This is not your condemnation. This is your call to come out. To come home. To come alive.

So, rise, remnant. Say it with fire:

"I am not ashamed of the eternal Gospel, alive with Heaven's thunder and urgency! I will live it. I will preach it. I will walk in it. And I will never bow to Babylon again!"

This is the final separation. This is your moment of no return. Walk out. Stand up. Shout loud. The King is calling - and you are the answer.

Scripture References:
- Galatians 1:8
- 2 Corinthians 6:14
- Matthew 7:21
- Romans 1:16
- Revelation 3:16
- Jeremiah 1:5
- John 10:27
- Psalm 89:34

Bonus: Chapter Seventeen

Obedience To God VS Man

Obedience to God Alone: Rejecting the Counterfeit Authority of Men

From the first words of Genesis to the final amen of Revelation, the Bible resounds with a commanding theme: God alone is to be obeyed. His authority is unshakable, His decrees are holy, and His Word is final. Yet, time and again, human leaders have attempted to usurp the place of God by demanding obedience that belongs solely to Him. This is not merely error - it is rebellion. Scripture warns us not to give men what is reserved for God. Obedience that contradicts God's will is disobedience in disguise.

Obedience to the Voice of God is Non-Negotiable

God has always demanded personal, direct obedience to His voice. Israel's very identity was rooted in hearing and obeying God's command. When Moses prepared them for blessing, he set the condition plainly:

"*And it shall come to pass, if thou shalt hearken diligently unto the voice of the LORD thy God, to observe and to do all his commandments which I command thee this day, that the LORD thy God will set thee on high above all nations of the earth."* (Deuteronomy 28:1)

This was not a suggestion, and it did not include obedience to religious leaders who deviated from God's voice. King Saul learned this painfully when he obeyed the people instead of God:

"And Samuel said, Hath the LORD as great delight in burnt offerings and sacrifices, as in obeying the voice of the LORD? Behold, to obey is better than sacrifice, and to hearken than the fat of rams." (1 Samuel 15:22)

When men set themselves up as the voice of God but lead contrary to His Word, following them becomes rebellion against the very God we claim to serve.

Jesus Christ Exposed False Authority

Jesus never exalted religious titles or positional authority. Instead, He exposed it. The Pharisees and scribes claimed divine authority while contradicting the will of God. Jesus warned:

"The scribes and the Pharisees sit in Moses' seat: All therefore whatsoever they bid you observe, that observe and do; but do not ye after their works: for they say, and do not." (Matthew 23:2-3)

He makes clear that their actions were corrupt, and their authority had become hollow. They preached, but they did not practice. Their leadership was rooted in pride:

"But all their works they do for to be seen of men... And love the uppermost rooms at feasts... and to be called of men, Rabbi, Rabbi." (Matthew 23:5-7)

Jesus then deconstructs their system:

"But be not ye called Rabbi: for one is your Master, even Christ; and all ye are brethren... Neither be ye called masters: for one is your Master, even Christ." (Matthew 23:8, 10)

Christ's words strip religious leaders of any assumed authority not rooted in divine obedience. To follow them when they oppose God's commands is to deny Christ's lordship.

Apostolic Teachings Demand Testing of Leaders

The apostles understood the danger of blind obedience. Paul rebuked the Corinthian church for elevating personalities over principle:

"For while one saith, I am of Paul; and another, I am of Apollos; are ye not carnal?" (1 Corinthians 3:4)

He called them to imitate him only to the degree he mirrored Christ:

"Be ye followers of me, even as I also am of Christ." (1 Corinthians 11:1)

Leaders are not infallible. Scripture commands all believers to test:

"Beloved, believe not every spirit, but try the spirits whether they are of God: because many false prophets are gone out into the world." (1 John 4:1)

The Bereans were praised for evaluating Paul himself:

"These were more noble... in that they received the word with all readiness of mind, and searched the scriptures daily, whether those things were so." (Acts 17:11)

True apostles encourage scrutiny. Only false teachers fear biblical examination.

When Obeying Men Means Disobeying God

The earliest disciples faced religious orders to stop preaching Christ. They didn't hesitate:

"Then Peter and the other apostles answered and said, We ought to obey God rather than men." (Acts 5:29)

This isn't a secondary principle - it is central to the Christian life. When a leader, denomination, or pastor teaches contrary to Scripture, obedience to them is treason against God. Silence in the face of falsehood is complicity.

Man-Made Leadership Tests Are an Abomination

Churches today often elevate leaders through unscriptural processes - interviews, politics, financial influence, and man-made qualifications. But Scripture gives us God's criteria:

"Look not on his countenance, or on the height of his stature... for man looketh on the outward appearance, but the LORD looketh on the heart." (1 Samuel 16:7)

It is the Holy Spirit, not a committee, who appoints:

"*Take heed therefore unto yourselves, and to all the flock, over the which the Holy Ghost hath made you overseers...*" (Acts 20:28)

Paul outlines the only legitimate qualifications:

"*If a man desire the office of a bishop, he desireth a good work. A bishop then must be blameless, the husband of one wife, vigilant, sober... apt to teach.*" (1 Timothy 3:1-2)

No board vote, academic degree, or denominational approval can replace God's method. When churches create their own leadership tests, they reject the government of God.

Obeying God Means Defying False Authority

God is calling His people back to obedience - not to men, not to institutions, but to His voice and Word. Jesus alone is the Head of the Church (Colossians 1:18). When men seek to replace Him, they become idols. When churches demand allegiance above Scripture, they become Babylon.

Obedience to God means speaking truth when it is dangerous, rejecting leaders when they are corrupt, and living holy even when misunderstood. The remnant God is raising will not bow to religious tyranny. They will be uncompromising, discerning, and Spirit-led.

Let our confession be rooted in the Word:

"*Therefore, my beloved brethren, be ye stedfast, unmoveable, always abounding in the work of the Lord...*" (1 Corinthians 15:58)

And let our allegiance be firm:

"*...choose you this day whom ye will serve... but as for me and my house, we will serve the LORD.*" (Joshua 24:15)

This is the obedience that heaven demands. This is the obedience that hell fears.

Warning to the Remnant:

Beware the pastor who positions themselves as the god of your destiny - controlling your decisions, demanding blind allegiance, and disguising manipulation as divine authority. When a leader requires 100% loyalty to their own errors, their private sins, and their public mistakes - run. You are not under covenant - you are under control. That is not shepherding; that is spiritual slavery. Flee from such places. Flee from pulpits that pretend to be thrones.

Because pastors are still human. They bleed. They battle. They wrestle with lust, pride, and insecurity just like anyone else. They are not infallible. They are not your king. They are not your Holy Spirit. And when they fall - and many do - it is not your responsibility to carry the weight of their deception cloaked in "honor." Your first loyalty is not to the one with the microphone; it is to the One with the nail-scarred hands.

Do not be seduced by charisma without character, gifting without governance, or sermons that silence your discernment. The eternal gospel does not require you to lose your mind to keep your membership. Where the Spirit of the Lord is, there is liberty (2 Corinthians 3:17). And any place that chains your voice, your future, and your soul to a man instead of to the King - is Babylon in disguise.

Glossary

of Theological Terms

Condemnation

Definition: The state of being declared guilty or morally wrong due to sin. It provokes a sense of accountability essential for spiritual correction.

Biblical Support:

John 3:18: *"Whoever believes in him is not condemned, but whoever does not believe is condemned already..."*

Romans 8:1: *"There is therefore now no condemnation for those who are in Christ Jesus."*

Clarification: Condemnation from God is reserved for those outside of Christ. Conviction, not condemnation, is what believers experience to lead them to repentance (John 16:8).

Flesh (Lust of the Flesh)

Definition: The carnal nature of humanity that craves sinful gratification, often through physical or emotional pleasure at the expense of spiritual obedience.

Biblical Support:

Galatians 5:17: *"For the desires of the flesh are against the Spirit..."*
1 John 2:16: *"For all that is in the world—the desires of the flesh and the desires of the eyes and pride of life—is not from the Father but is from the world."*

Clarification: Lust is a function of the flesh, and the term "flesh" encompasses more than sexual sin; it refers to the fallen nature in opposition to God.

Gospel of Healing
Definition: Not a standalone gospel in Scripture. Healing is a benefit of the Kingdom, not the message itself.
Biblical Clarification:
Healing accompanies the gospel of the Kingdom (Matthew 4:23), but is not a separate gospel message.

Gospel of Heaven
Definition: Often confused with the Gospel of the Kingdom. Biblically synonymous in some teachings, but the "Gospel of the Kingdom" is the actual terminology used by Jesus.
Biblical Support:

Matthew 4:17: *"Repent, for the kingdom of heaven is at hand."*

Luke 4:43: *"I must preach the good news of the kingdom of God..."*

Clarification: "Heaven" refers to the domain; the message is about God's rulership.

Gospel of Salvation

Definition: Not explicitly labeled in Scripture as a gospel. Salvation is a benefit/result of the Gospel of the Kingdom.

Biblical Clarification:

The term is not found in Scripture as a separate gospel. See Romans 1:16: *"...the gospel... is the power of God for salvation..."*

Gospel of the Kingdom

Definition: The only gospel that Jesus and His apostles preached—declaring the rulership of God, calling people to repent and come under His reign.

Biblical Support:

Matthew 24:14: *"This gospel of the kingdom will be preached in all the world..."*

Galatians 1:8: *"...if we or an angel from heaven should preach to you a gospel contrary... let him be accursed."*

Clarification: This is the central message of the New Testament.

Gospel of Wealth/Prosperity

Definition: A man-made distortion of the gospel that equates material gain with spiritual approval. It is not found in Scripture.

Biblical Clarification:

1 Timothy 6:5: "...*supposing that godliness is a means of gain.*"

Luke 12:15: "...*one's life does not consist in the abundance of his possessions.*"

Conclusion: Prosperity gospel contradicts Jesus' teachings about suffering and self-denial.

Grace

Definition: Unmerited divine favor—receiving blessings not earned.

Biblical Support:

Ephesians 2:8-9: "*For by grace you have been saved through faith...*"

Clarification: Grace is not something you "deserve," but something given freely despite unworthiness.

Holiness

Definition: A life set apart from sin and consecrated for God's purposes; a state of moral purity and spiritual distinction.

Biblical Support:

1 Peter 1:16: *"Be holy, for I am holy."*
Hebrews 12:14: *"...without holiness no one will see the Lord."*

Clarification: Holiness is internal transformation, not external rituals or appearances.

Holy

Definition: Anything set apart by God for sacred use.

Biblical Support:

Exodus 3:5: *"...the place on which you are standing is holy ground."*

Clarification: Holiness is about divine purpose and consecration, not merely moral perfection.

Mercy

Definition: Withholding deserved punishment as an act of compassion.

Biblical Support:

Titus 3:5: *"He saved us... according to his own mercy..."*

Psalm 103:10: *"He does not deal with us according to our sins..."*

Repentance (Greek: metanoia)

Definition:

Repentance is a Spirit-led change of mind about sin that results in turning completely away from it—never to return—and aligning one's life with God's will.

Biblical Support:

Acts 2:38: *"Repent and be baptized... for the forgiveness of your sins."*

Hebrews 6:1: *"...the elementary doctrine of Christ... repentance from dead works and of faith toward God..."*

Clarification: A decisive, Spirit-empowered change of mind that produces a complete turning away from sin, self, and the world toward God. It involves acknowledging sin as rebellion, feeling godly sorrow (2 Corinthians 7:10), and intentionally choosing a new direction aligned with righteousness, never returning to the former way of life (Luke 15:7; Acts 3:19). True repentance is not merely emotional regret but a transformation of the will and behavior rooted in faith (Matthew 3:8; Romans 2:4).

Shame

Definition: A mental and emotional state of perceived unworthiness or defectiveness, often contrary to the redemptive work of Christ.

Biblical Support:

Romans 10:11: *"Whoever believes in him will not be put to shame."*
Hebrews 12:2: *"...despising the shame..."*

Clarification: God's plan is to remove shame and restore identity in Christ.

Sin

Definition: Any act, thought, or motive that violates God's will or law, whether Old or New Testament.

Biblical Support:

1 John 3:4: *"Sin is lawlessness."*
James 4:17: *"...to him who knows to do good and does not do it, to him it is sin."*

Clarification: Sin is not just action but also motive and omission. NT believers are still responsible to God's moral law.

Spirit of the Age

Definition: A cultural atmosphere shaped by demonic influence that normalizes rebellion against God's truth.

Biblical Support:

Ephesians 2:2: *"...the prince of the power of the air, the spirit... at work in the sons of disobedience."*

Romans 12:2: *"Do not be conformed to this world..."*

Start of the Born Again Process

Definition: Initiated by faith and repentance—confessing sin and turning to Christ, but requires ongoing obedience.

Biblical Support:

Acts 2:38: *"Repent and be baptized... for the forgiveness of your sins."*

Hebrews 6:1: *"...the elementary doctrine of Christ... repentance from dead works and of faith toward God..."*

Clarification: Salvation is not secured by a single prayer but through enduring faith.

Index

Thematic

Babylon and Mixture
Concepts tied to spiritual compromise, deception, rebellion, and the counterfeit systems of Babylon.

Deliverance
Key words relating to spiritual liberation, freedom from demonic oppression, and the ministry of setting captives free.

Jesus Christ
Names and titles related to the person and work of Jesus, including redemptive and messianic references.

Kingdom Authority
Terms that emphasize divine government, spiritual dominion, and the believer's position of rulership under Christ.

Obedience and Repentance
Keywords addressing the call to surrender, turn from sin, and align fully with God's commands.

Remnant and Boldness
Language used to describe the rising remnant, spiritual courage, and unwavering faith in hostile environments.

Separation and Holiness
Terms reflecting sanctification, purity, consecration, and distinction from worldly systems.

Shame and Identity

Words centered on healing from shame, restoration of identity, and revelation of sonship in Christ.

Truth and Gospel

Words connected to the eternal gospel, proclamation of truth, and bold preaching of the Kingdom.

Voice of God

Language that reflects God's speaking nature, prophetic utterances, and the power of divine command.

Babylon And Mixture
- Babylon, 3, 4, 1, 2, 3, 5, 7, 8, 9, 10, 11, 15, 16, 21, 22, 23, 24, 25, 26, 27, 28, 29, 30, 31, 41, 42, 49, 58, 62, 64, 65, 66, 67, 68, 70, 71, 72, 75, 76, 78, 80, 82, 83, 84, 85, 86, 88, 89, 90, 91, 92, 93, 94, 95, 99, 101, 109, 110, 111, 112, 113, 114, 115, 116, 117, 118, 119, 120, 121, 125, 126, 127, 130, 135, 137
- Compromise, 2, 6, 8, 9, 11, 18, 21, 23, 25, 31, 39, 46, 61, 70, 74, 75, 78, 80, 85, 86, 93, 107, 110, 116, 117, 119, 121, 124, 125, 128, 129, 146
- Confusion, 5, 21, 100, 107, 110, 111, 117, 119
- Culture, 14, 17, 22, 25, 27, 65, 70, 91, 92, 113, 117, 120
- Deception, 6, 7, 8, 14, 21, 22, 41, 43, 52, 62, 66, 69, 83, 126, 136, 146
- False, 1, 2, 5, 11, 16, 18, 26, 35, 41, 83, 86, 88, 89, 90, 91, 93, 95, 98, 132, 133, 134, 135
- Idolatry, 13, 5, 22, 25, 74, 110
- Mixture, 22, 25, 31, 47, 88, 92
- Rebellion, 5, 18, 22, 47, 57, 60, 65, 66, 69, 74, 110, 117, 118, 129, 131, 132, 143, 145, 146

Deliverance

Break, 1, 14, 23, 31, 38,
42, 51, 60, 78, 83, 84,
86, 87, 93, 101, 105,
127, 129
Breaks, 6, 14, 41, 62, 70,
82, 85, 89, 91, 93, 100,
128
Cast, 8, 25, 26, 27, 31, 38,
39, 51, 56, 59, 60, 61,
62, 65, 72, 85, 105, 106,
107, 109, 110, 113, 116
Chains, 41, 57, 62, 82, 90,
105, 137
Deliverance, 8, 17, 19, 24,
37, 51, 56, 57, 58, 60,
62, 80, 90, 105, 106,
108, 113, 122
Demonic, 15, 58
Demons, 10, 17, 19, 24,
38, 42, 47, 51, 56, 57,
58, 59, 60, 61, 62, 76,
79, 80, 93, 100, 105,
106, 116, 119
Evict, 38, 57
Evicted, 98
Eviction, 58, 60, 84
Freedom, 2, 39, 56, 58, 60,
61, 62, 82, 111, 113, 146
Oppression, 58, 60, 70,
146
Strongman, 15, 59
Jesus Christ
Blood, 19, 22, 27, 37, 42,
67, 77, 78, 97, 104, 106,
111, 129
Christ, 7, 18, 9, 11, 14, 15,
16, 22, 34, 35, 37, 42,
47, 79, 84, 91, 92, 98,
106, 108, 111, 113, 120,
127, 132, 133, 134, 138,
143, 144, 145, 146, 147
Cross, 6, 15, 17, 25, 36,
38, 41, 52, 79, 98, 112,
125, 129
Jesus, 7, 14, 15, 18, 7, 8, 9,
10, 11, 14, 15, 16, 17,
18, 19, 22, 24, 27, 35,
36, 37, 38, 43, 44, 45,
46, 47, 49, 50, 51, 52,
53, 54, 56, 57, 58, 59,
61, 65, 66, 67, 68, 69,
71, 75, 76, 77, 88, 89,
90, 91, 92, 96, 97, 98,
99, 103, 104, 105, 106,
112, 119, 120,121, 125,
126, 128, 132, 133, 135,
138, 139, 140, 141, 146
Lamb, 75, 76, 78, 106,
121, 125
Resurrection, 9, 43, 52, 96,
118
Savior, 15, 50, 66, 68, 125
Kingdom Authority
Ambassador, 94
Ambassadors, 13, 71, 108,
109
Authority, 9, 10, 12, 13,
17, 19, 23, 27, 31, 35,
38, 39, 56, 59, 60, 65,
68, 69, 71, 79, 80, 86,
93, 97, 99, 101, 103,
104, 105, 107, 108, 109,
111, 112, 115, 116, 117,

148

120, 121, 122, 124, 131, 132, 133, 136
Dominion, 15, 50, 70, 83, 103, 104, 109, 125, 128, 146
Govern, 13, 103, 109
Government, 14, 50, 51, 83
Jurisdiction, 70, 93, 95, 106, 107, 108, 120
Kingdom, 4, 7, 13, 14, 16, 17, 2, 3, 5, 9, 10, 11, 12, 13, 15, 16, 17, 23, 24, 25, 26, 27, 31, 38, 39, 41, 42, 43, 44, 45, 46, 47, 49, 50, 51, 52, 54, 55, 56, 57, 58, 60, 62, 64, 65, 66, 67, 68, 69, 70, 71, 72, 75, 77, 79, 80, 82, 84, 86, 87, 88, 89, 90, 91, 93, 94, 95, 96, 98, 99, 101, 103, 104, 105, 106, 107, 108, 109, 111, 112, 113, 114, 115, 116, 119, 120, 122, 124, 125, 126, 128, 139, 140, 146, 147
Reign, 9, 11, 44, 62, 79, 86, 91, 92, 104, 118, 140
Rule, 6, 7, 10, 11, 21, 22, 27, 42, 47, 51, 64, 67, 84

Obedience And Repentance

Align, 9, 17, 42, 78, 86, 93, 127, 129, 146
Alignment, 11, 13, 19, 41, 42, 45, 50, 54, 60, 64, 65, 66, 69, 70, 72, 82,
91, 96, 98, 99, 105, 106, 116
Forsake, 10
Obedience, 9, 8, 10, 16, 23, 25, 43, 45, 53, 54, 61, 64, 66, 67, 68, 69, 70, 72, 75, 82, 106, 111, 113, 119, 131, 132, 133, 134, 135, 136, 138, 145
Repentance, 16, 17, 23, 25, 43, 44, 46, 79, 82, 83, 85, 86, 87, 89, 111, 115, 117, 119, 138, 143, 145
Return, 1, 2, 10, 17, 54, 61, 85, 101, 115, 118, 121, 130, 143
Submit, 11, 64, 72, 127
Surrender, 5, 7, 9, 14, 25, 30, 39, 43, 47, 51, 54, 55, 66, 67, 68, 78, 79, 82, 83, 86, 128, 129, 146
Yield, 66, 86, 96

Remnant And Boldness

Bold, 14, 19, 34, 37, 39, 42, 78, 99, 127, 147
Boldly, 3, 13, 37, 55, 108
Boldness, 11, 18, 19, 27, 31, 55, 78, 92, 99, 108, 109, 115
Courage, 2, 27, 78, 146
Courageous, 19, 94
Remnant, 8, 11, 22, 28, 31, 54, 64, 66, 74, 75, 76, 77, 78, 79, 80, 86, 92, 94, 109, 113, 115, 116, 118, 127, 130, 135, 146

Rise, 13, 31, 33, 37, 39,
54, 72, 75, 80, 86, 87,
94, 101, 104, 106, 107,
109, 115, 116, 122, 130
Stand, 11, 18, 31, 34, 37,
77, 93, 94, 112, 114, 116
Unashamed, 11, 19, 47, 58,
93, 127

Separation And Holiness
Clean, 26, 70, 84, 86, 104
Consecarted, 70, 122, 142
Holiness, 17, 25, 43, 70,
71, 75, 79, 82, 93, 112,
113, 115, 118
Holy, 11, 24, 25, 27, 30,
43, 49, 54, 55, 70, 71,
86, 91, 92, 100, 103,
105, 113, 115, 121, 129,
131, 135, 136, 142
Pure, 114, 122
Righteous, 46, 84, 99, 104
Righteousness, 2, 36, 39,
45, 70, 83, 107, 118,
120, 125, 143
Sanctified, 128
Separate, 91, 115, 118,
139, 140
Separation, 70, 92, 119,
128, 129, 130

Shame And Identity
Beloved, 38, 49, 69, 99,
129, 135
Condemnation, 38, 39, 43,
120, 130, 138
Identity, 2, 5, 6, 33, 34, 38,
46, 47, 69, 75, 95, 96,
98, 99, 100, 101, 105,
115, 118, 120, 121, 131,
144, 147
Orphan, 96, 97
Rejection, 35, 96, 97
Renewed, 120
Restoration, 3, 9, 15, 17,
43, 96, 100, 147
Shame, 1, 2, 3, 7, 10, 11,
16, 18, 19, 31, 33, 34,
35, 36, 37, 38, 39, 42,
43, 57, 59, 60, 75, 78,
86, 87, 89, 95, 99, 100,
101, 115, 120, 128, 129,
144, 147
Sonship, 95, 96, 98, 100,
147

Truth And Gospel
Declare, 9, 11, 15, 37, 39,
55, 60, 62, 65, 78, 83,
92, 93, 98, 105, 106,
107, 108, 127
Declares, 2, 13, 26, 30, 35,
42, 51, 53, 65, 70, 71,
75, 84, 86, 96, 99, 100,
101, 107, 109, 114, 117,
120, 121, 129
Eternal, 11, 13, 16, 35, 37,
39, 52, 57, 58, 59, 62,
68, 76, 77, 78, 79, 80,
82, 88, 89, 92, 93, 100,
106, 109, 111, 124, 125,
127, 129, 130, 136, 147
Gospel, 13, 16, 6, 8, 9, 10,
11, 12, 13, 14, 15, 16,
17, 18, 19, 20, 22, 23,
24, 34, 35, 37, 39, 41,
42, 43, 44, 46, 47, 48,

50, 52, 53, 54, 56, 57, 58, 59, 62, 65, 66, 67, 72, 76, 77, 78, 79, 80, 82, 83, 84, 88, 89, 90, 91, 92, 93, 94, 96, 98, 100, 103, 105, 106, 109, 111, 112, 113, 121, 122, 124, 125, 127, 128, 129, 130, 136, 139, 140, 141, 147

Message, 8, 16, 17, 18, 34, 35, 42, 44, 48, 67, 77, 83, 89, 90, 112, 125, 128, 139, 140, 141

Preach, 10, 13, 16, 18, 23, 35, 42, 43, 52, 56, 65, 78, 80, 90, 92, 94, 105, 106, 111, 113, 124, 130, 140

Proclaim, 2, 12, 56

Real, 13, 16, 8, 18, 42, 66, 83, 89, 90, 91, 100, 115

Truth, 5, 6, 7, 9, 10, 11, 13, 17, 18, 22, 24, 25, 27, 28, 35, 43, 44, 45, 52, 57, 59, 61, 62, 77, 78, 79, 87, 88, 89, 90, 91, 93, 94, 100, 109, 111, 112, 115, 117, 118, 119, 124, 126, 129, 135, 145, 147

Voice Of God

Call, 19, 44, 47, 50, 53, 67, 71, 80, 82, 86, 92, 95, 105, 113, 115, 116, 118, 119, 130, 146

Called, 9, 13, 14, 16, 26, 41, 51, 59, 60, 70, 80, 82, 84, 89, 93, 95, 98, 106, 119, 120, 125, 133

Command, 31, 131, 132, 147

Commanded, 29, 51, 67

Decree, 11, 14, 15, 48, 54, 101, 106, 129

Instruction, 53, 64

Speak, 8, 12, 13, 18, 34, 36, 37, 44, 48, 49, 53, 54, 59, 65, 72, 87, 94, 105, 106, 108, 109, 118

Speaks, 5, 14, 35, 49, 50, 51, 53, 129

Thunder, 12, 35, 37, 39, 48, 52, 57, 59, 62, 76, 78, 79, 80, 82, 88, 89, 92, 93, 106, 109, 111, 122, 124, 125, 127, 129, 130

Thundered, 14, 56, 117

Voice, 6, 17, 33, 34, 35, 38, 39, 41, 42, 49, 50, 51, 52, 53, 54, 55, 58, 59, 60, 62, 71, 72, 74, 76, 77, 85, 86, 93, 96, 101, 105, 106, 108, 117, 119, 121, 122, 125, 129, 131, 132, 135, 137

Word, 14, 9, 17, 34, 36, 42, 43, 44, 50, 51, 53, 54, 55, 60, 61, 65, 67, 68, 71, 72, 78, 88, 89, 91, 92, 97, 99, 106, 117, 129, 131, 132, 134, 135

Words, 7, 56, 61, 77, 117, 131, 133, 146

Scripture Index

Old Testament

Genesis
1:28 .... 103, 109
3:1 .... 5, 11, 72
3:1-10 39
3:7-10 36
11:4 .... 21, 31
Exodus
3:5 142
3:10 .... 119, 123
20:19 .... 12, 20, 49, 55
Deuteronomy
14:1 .... 97, 102
28:1 132
Joshua
24:15 136
Judges
7:7 81
1 Samuel
3:10 .... 54, 55
8:5 .... 7, 11
15:22 .... 72, 73, 132
16:7 134
1 Kings
18:21 122
18:30-39 .... 119, 122
19:18 75
2 Kings
17:7-18 2
Job
22:28 108
22:28 109
Psalms

26:1-2 20
34:5 .... 39, 101, 102
68:6 .... 97, 102
89:34 .... 129, 130
103:10 143
137:4 .... 23, 31
139:23-24 .... 28, 32, 87
Proverbs
23:7 .... 35, 40
28:1 .... 99, 102
29:18 14
Song of Solomon
Song of Songs 6:3 123
Song of Songs 8:6 122, 123
Isaiah
1:9 .... 74, 80
1:13-17 .... 26, 32
1:16-17 .... 84, 87
9:2 1
43:1 .... 98, 102
50:7 .... 101, 102
52:11 .... 114, 116
53:5 .... 37, 39
56:4-5 2
58:12 .... 96, 102, 107, 109, 120, 123
61:1 2
61:7 .... 37, 39, 100, 101
61:10 .... 120, 123
Jeremiah
1:5 .... 128, 130
1:10 .... 106, 109

23:29 .... 89, 94
Ezekiel
18:30 .... 83, 87
22:26 .... 25, 32
Daniel
2-5 31
3:16 2
18,6:10 2

Joel
2:1 .... 115, 116
2:12-13 .... 76, 81
2:25 .... 121, 123
Amos
3:3 .... 91, 94
8:11 .... 117, 122

New Testament

Matthew
3:8 .... 85, 87, 143
3:17 38, 39, 69, 72, 99, 101
4:10 20
4:17 20, 50, 55, 67, 72, 140
4:23 139
5:8 123
5:8) 122
6:10 .... 51, 55
6:22-23 20
6:33 .... 13, 20, 80, 116
7:21 .. 10, 11, 48, 112, 116, 126, 130
7:24 .... 69, 72
10:34 .... 17, 20, 88, 94
12:43-45 .... 61, 63
15:8 .... 48, 65, 72
15:8-9 .... 24, 32
16:18 81
16:19 .... 107, 109
23:2-3 132
23:5-7 133
23:8 133
23:10 133
23:27 .... 44, 48
24:13 81
24:14 140
25 122
25:1-13 123

Mark
1:23-26 .... 58, 63
1:27 .... 105, 109
3:27 .... 59, 63

4:39 .... 51, 55
5:1-15 58
16:17 .... 56, 62

Luke
4:18 .... 56, 57, 62
4:43 140
6:26 .. 8, 11, 18, 20, 44, 48, 81
6:46 .... 48, 67, 72
9:23 .... 20, 47, 48
9:35 55
9:62 80
10:19 .... 81, 99, 101
11:20 .... 51, 55, 57, 62
11:28 .... 72, 73
12:15 141
12:51 .... 89, 90, 94
15:7 143
15:11-32 .... 117, 122
15:20-24 102
15:22 120
17:21 .... 103, 109

John
1:12 .... 97, 101
3:3 45
3:3-5 48
3:5 46
3:18 138
6:66-69 .... 77, 80
8:11 .... 35, 39
8:36 39
10:27 .... 53, 55, 129, 130
11:43 .... 51, 55

14:6 .... 52, 55	10:21 .... 119, 122
14:15 .... 67, 72	11:1 133
15:15 102	15:31 87
16:8 138	15:58 135
17:17 .... 91, 94	**2 Corinthians**
20:21 .... 104, 109	2:15 .... 79, 81
Acts	3:17 .... 62, 137
1:8 .... 104, 109	5:17 .... 36, 40, 98, 101
2:38 .... 143, 145	5:20 .... 108, 109
3:19 .... 82, 87, 143	6:14 .... 125, 130
4:29-31 80	6:17 .... 81, 118, 122
5:29 134	7:10 ..... 33, 40, 85, 87, 143
13:2-3 81	8:9 .... 37, 40
17:11 134	10:4-5 .... 110, 116
20:28 135	10:5 87
Romans	**Galatians**
1:16 .. 9, 11, 15, 17, 20, 34, 39, 42, 48, 80, 84, 87, 92, 94, 113, 116, 127, 130, 140	1:8 .... 124, 130, 140
	1:8-9 .... 10, 11, 20, 80
	4:6 101
	4:16 .... 90, 94
2:4 143	5:1 .... 39, 81
8:1 ... 35, 39, 120, 123, 138	5:16 .... 43, 61, 63
8:11 .... 96, 101	5:17 139
8:15 .... 39, 40, 97, 101	**Ephesians**
8:19 13, 104, 109, 121, 123	1:5 .... 98, 101
8:37 109	2:2 145
10:9 .... 67, 72	2:8-9 141
10:10 45	4:27 .... 38, 40
10:11 144	5:25-27 20
11:4 .... 75, 81	5:27 .... 81, 121, 123
11:5 .... 74, 80	6:12 .... 27, 32, 111, 116
12:2 . 26, 32, 112, 116, 145	6:13 .... 93, 94
14:17 .... 13, 20, 116	6:19-20 81
16:17 .... 92, 94	**Philippians**
1 Corinthians	1:29 81
3:4 133	3:13-14 .... 39, 40
4:20 .... 20, 60, 63	3:20 .... 107, 109
	Colossians

1:18 135
2:14-15 .... 38, 40
2:15 36
1 Timothy
3:1-2 135
6:5 141
2 Timothy
1:7 80
3:5 .... 37, 40
4:2-5 81
4:3 .... 24, 32
Titus
3:5 143
Hebrews
3:16-19 .... 114, 116
4:12 .... 51, 55
5:9 .... 68, 72
6:1 .... 83, 87, 143, 145
11:38 .... 77, 80
12:2 .... 36, 39, 144
12:14 142
12:27 .... 114, 116
12:28-29 .... 31, 32
James
1:22 .... 54, 55
4:4 .... 23, 32, 119, 122
4:7 .... 105, 109
4:17 144

1 Peter
1:14-15 .... 70, 72
1:16 142
2:9 ..... 36, 40, 81, 100, 102
1 John
2:6 .... 71, 73
2:16 139
3:1 .... 98, 101
3:4 144
3:8 .... 58, 62
4:1 133
5:7-8 .... 42, 48
Revelation
1:15 55
2:7 .... 53, 55
2:10 37
3:2-3 .... 118, 123
3:16 .... 128, 130
3:19 .... 86, 87
12:10 .... 34, 39
12:11 .... 78, 106, 109
14:4 .... 76, 81
17:1-6 .... 22, 31
18:2 .... 30, 31
18:2-4 .... 114, 116
18:4 .... 31, 80
19:7 ... 20, 75, 80, 121, 123
22:17 .... 122, 123